WALLA WALLA Sweet

Edmond Bruneau

 Published by Boston Books - www.bostonbooks.org

ISBN: 978-1-936769-03-2
Library of Congress Control Number: 2021919762

Cover Design: Edmond Bruneau
Editor: Donna Lange

Previous books by Edmond Bruneau
Prescription for Advertising - 1986
Colors of My Within - 2011
New Hues and Past Tales - 2016
The Totem - 2018

Lyricist for the songs of Robot Raven
Robot Raven's Greatest Hits - Part One - 2015
Robot Raven's Greatest Hits - Part Two - 2016
Life Goes On - 2017
Set to Soar - 2018
Robot Raven Rockers - 2018
Kick Back Relax - 2020
(songs from the mellow side of Robot Raven)

For Cory Bentz and Randy Grant
who became our first new friends
to welcome us to Walla Walla.

Also, special thanks to all the members
of the Walla Walla Pickleball Association
and the Jazzercise Walla Walla Center
who went out of their way
to make us feel like we were home.

photo by Donna Lange

The author enjoying a glass of wine at a local Walla Walla winery

FORWARD

I would not wish the task of selling one's home, building a new place three hours away and moving onto anyone.

The poem in which the book is titled – *Walla Walla Swee*t – can be located on page 11. The two poems prior seemed to be important to precede it. *Find Your Tribe* is about exploring and uncovering the best place to live for you. *Reason, No Rhyme* explains my reality of being far too overwhelmed to do any serious writing – and looking forward to beginning again in a new community and getting my poetic chops back after the hiatus.

It's also important to note that after only six months of settling in Walla Walla, the Covid-19 pandemic began. The poems I wrote about it, dated and in chronological order, can be found in a special section of the book starting on page 151.

Special recognition again to Donna Lange, who is the first to read each poem and the person who makes them better.

TABLE OF CONTENTS

Poems of the Pandemic

Find Your Tribe

There is a tribe for you, somewhere.
A place where you belong.
A place where many share a point of view.
A place that sings the same song.

We seek to live in harmony.
We seek to live in peace.
Find our subjective safety net.
Watch our friends increase.

They say it takes a village
to raise a single child.
Perhaps, no matter what our age,
we're more tribal than we're wild.

Nothing is ever perfect,
on that we can agree.
Some places are better than others, though,
for one's own particular journey.

Perhaps the city is not for you.
Or rural's not your thing.
Smell the salty ocean air
or the desert in the spring.

It's yours to find, this special place.
It will not come to you.
The world waits to be explored –
it pleads to be pursued.

Seek out your captivating colony.
Seek out your therapeutic tribe.
The journey may take a lifetime.
Let discovery be your guide.

Reason, No Rhyme

This may be the last poem I write
until we settle in after the move.

Perhaps I'll find other poetry enthusiasts
who'll share my passion
and are keen about discussing
our latest weekly output.

So, this one better be profound.
At the very least, distinguished.

Stepping out of the spotlight
and into shadows of my soul
surely will be a surreal experience.
Between selling one home
and moving into another,
my poetry brain will be on sabbatical.

Like an old discarded car,
it might require a charged battery
and some new spark plugs
to get the jalopy rolling again.

I promise not to leave it
abandoned out front –
rusting and decaying into
a neighborhood eyesore.

I will restore it to vintage condition
and make it a daily driver.
Or at the very least,
take it out for a spin
a couple times a week.

Fact is, I enjoy the drive.
It's not a task, but a pleasure.
Which is why I will continue
to pick up where I left off
after the chaos diminishes
and the dust settles.

June 23, 2019

Walla Walla Sweet

Peel back layers
of the onion.
So much more
than meets
the naked eye.

Rain Shadow.
Rich earth.
Place of Many Waters.
Palouse hills.
Blue Mountains.

Downtown beckons
charm of yesterday past.
Brick and mortar.
Old becomes new again.
Preserved renaissance.

Place to grow.
Wheat and wine.
Home and heart.
Young minds
cultivate here.

More town than city.
Friendly village
with language of
smiles and satisfaction.
Slow down and savor.

It's where we chose
to spend our later years –
nurtured by the area's
old growth gentle giants.
Time to branch out.

They say you can't go back
to the halcyon days of youth.
Innocent, happy times
suddenly rhyme and reappear.
Walla Walla. Sweet.

No Matter What

We think of love
as a warm breeze
with blue skies,
twinkling eyes,
smiles and laughter.
Holding hands
and soft caress,
embracing sunset after.

Such moments don't define
the way I think of you.
There can also be clouds,
cold winds and stormy weather.
The realistic way
to look at love,
no matter what,
it's there to share together.

In fact, that's when love
is most important when
things aren't easy,
painless or smooth.
Love binds us in the worst of times.
Pressures. Disasters. Failures.
Or simply when
benevolence is bruised.

No matter what we both go through.
No matter in light or darkness.
No matter if things are thick or thin
or one of us less dauntless –
My love for you is always there.
My heart will never shut.
My care is carried everywhere.
No matter what.
No matter what.
No matter what.

Let's Get Lost

Let's take a drive
into uncertainty.
Find a road
we've never traveled
to simply
see where it goes.
Let's get lost.

Maybe we'll find
an old country store
with horehound candy
in a counter jar.
Pick a pickle
right from the barrel.
Let's get lost.

We might find
a shortcut
not on any map.
Celebrate our discovery
and take the
old way back.
Let's get lost.

Cast aside the compass.
Resist the GPS.
Use your inner instinct.
Allow intuition to do the rest.
Curiosity and wonder –
truly your best companions.
Let's get lost.

Stay in control
wherever you go.
Leave nothing left
to chance.
Might be smart and prudent –
but where's the risk and romance?
Let's get lost.

Waterville Wedding

The late September weather
could not have been more perfect
for the beautiful country wedding.
Held in an abandoned church
with hay bales as our pews.
Young farm kids
beginning a new life together
with hope and promise in their eyes.
We didn't stay too long at the barn dance
after the bride and groom
kicked up their heels.
We escaped the celebration,
preferring to enjoy the
perfect dusk temperature
among the wheat, cattle and sagebrush.
Stayed close by in Coulee City
in a no-tell motel with its linoleum floor,
13-inch color television with one static channel
and vibrating double bed.
You, with a smile and warm spirit
embraced the farce with laughter.
I didn't know I could love you more,
but I did, just then.
Next day we headed home
with a tailwind and cloudy skies.
Chasing us, a haboob,
no more than 15 hours
after the wedding was over.
A wall of dust-filled darkness
marching forward like a blitzkrieg
toward certain armageddon.
A few hours sooner would have
shanghaied the simple country wedding
and sent us all packing for the hills.
We wouldn't have had fond memories
embracing the late summer evening
and laughing at our pathetic lodging.
And I would have had to wait longer
to fall even more in love with you.

Ed and Donna at the farm which hosted the Waterville wedding

The Waltz

It's a graceful dance we do.
A waltz best describes it.
Box step in the key of life.
Rising and falling with pivots.

We go through the motions
all in three-quarter time.
Face the fate that awaits us.
Mountains we must climb.

I'll try not to step on toes.
Or lead you far astray.
Deal with the world together
without getting in each other's way.

Luckily, we hear the same music.
Take our steps as one.
Waltz our way to our later years
until our dance is done.

Harley's Ghost

It's the fourth anniversary of my departure
and I wanted to tell you some things
I couldn't articulate back then.

First of all, you never told me I was a dog.
It was a little embarrassing to discover
I wasn't a cat. In fact, it was a calico
who rudely told me I was in the wrong line.

I know I barked instead of mewed.
And was a lot larger than the fifteen felines
that I lived with. But I just thought I was
a rare big barking cat breed. Guess not.

When the man left and didn't come back,
I came to live with you. You became my Alpha.
I know you were sad he was gone. Me too.
But I wanted to tell you just how great you were.

Loved the walks we took in the park.
In the hills. Even the wildlife refuge.
It was so hard for me to contain my excitement
in the car when we drove there.

I took you out in the weather during all seasons.
Sometimes I'd see you slip on the sidewalk ice.
Even though I had to be in the house all day,
I'd make sure you got some exercise after work.

When we moved by the river with the new fellow,
I didn't know what to think of him at first.
But he threw the ball for me every day
and we'd go out and pee by the fence together.

You were my mom and he was the step dad.
He'd take me down to the river and throw the
stick into it so I could bring it back. At first, I'd
swim out, retrieve it and he'd throw it again.

As time went on, it was more fun to leave him
on the shore while I pretended not to hear
his step dad commands.
He was just too easy to mess with.

Over time, I learned why you had chosen him.
He was kind and made you happy.
I grew to love him like you did.
I'm glad to see you are still together.

The day I died, I saw the water in your eyes
but I was too weak to worry about you.
I was in pain and my body wasn't cooperating.
You made the right decision to let me go.

Even though I did end up in the cat line.

Thank you for being such a wonderful mom.
I talk about you all the time and some of my
stories have the other dogs laughing in stitches.
Especially about step dad.

WASHINGTON

Harley with step dad. R.I.P. 2001 - 2015

Being in the Now

It's the journey, not the destination.
So the wise ones say, I suppose.
Being in the now, not then.
Being in the now, not the future.

We sit in our car or bus
or plane or train
and peer out the window
like watching a movie.
As a spectator, not a participant.
A blur of moving images
gathered up like a bouquet
and presented to the memory
as a token of
the time it took to get there.

If we were in the now,
we wouldn't observe through
the lens of glass –
but with wind in our hair,
scents in the air
and sounds of our propulsion
blending with the world at large.

But we move much too fast
with modern transportation
to be in the now.
It's the tradeoff we make
to get there quicker.
A time when we sacrifice now
and replace it with something
neither similar or satisfying.

Some souls travel through life
never realizing the disadvantage
of mankind's invention of speed –
for them, life is one blur after another.

An introspection derived
being in the now.

Look Closer

We give the world a glance –
enough to navigate our walk
or go about our busy day.
Look closer.
There are things
you haven't taken time to see.
Look closer.
At the sky.
See a cumulus alligator
or painted cirrus sunset.
Look closer.
At your feet.
A crack in cement
becomes an ant Oregon Trail.
Look closer.
You can make everyday
less ordinary
by simply looking
at what you already see
differently.
It just takes an extra,
precious moment.
Can you spare it
in a world where
there's never enough time?
Look closer
and give yourself the gift
of seeing beyond the blur
of daily existence.
Focus your cerebral camera –
flip the setting from auto to manual.
It's all there, waiting.
Look closer.

No One Gets Out Alive

Jim Morrison once said:
"No one gets out alive."
Ironic, since death means alive no longer.
The grim reaper. Eternal rest.

Maybe, if fortunate, we live on –
in our friends' hearts.
In our words
or art
or music
or kindness
we left behind before demise.

I read that sixty billion dollars
is spent annually
by the rich seeking earth eternity.
Curtail age. Cheat death.
Remain here, alive.

Life is a gift with an expiration date.
We all hope to live past it a bit
until, at least, things truly do go sour.
It's a suggested date, after all.
When it finally goes bad, we trash it.

Alive ones
left behind with bereavement
all taste what's to come
through gatherings and their grief.

No one gets out alive.
No one gets out and survives.
We cling to what we materialize,
not what we can't imagine.
it's our way to rationalize
our lives until we ashen.

Goodbye

I remember meeting you the first time
for lunch at our local Panera Bread®café.
Actually, on the way there,
just off the freeway exit,
the old sedan papered with bumper stickers,
tacky signs and peeling paint
pulled up next to me at the traffic light
with its turn signal blinking the opposite of mine –
and I'm thinking
"Thank God, he's not the weirdo I'm seeing".

I arrived first and procured a table for two.
Put my food order in. You were ten minutes late
because you had taken a wrong turn into the mall.
When you entered through the door I took
a wild guess and waved you over.
My food had just been delivered.
You asked, *"What's that?"* and ordered the same.
Your smile as you sat down revealed missing front
teeth and you sheepishly explained being in the midst
of dental work. Apologetic, actually.
I said, *"No problem"* with a gentle grin – but in the
back of my mind, I worried if you were homeless.

You asked me if there were any thrift shops close by,
as afternoon would be indulged by your compulsion.
We exchanged work and life histories and chatted
about our own love of poetry. Traded book for book.
Funny thing, it was me being interviewed
for an upcoming poetry reading you were organizing.
Guess I passed the audition.

Then today, a couple years later, I read a beautiful
ramble you wrote explaining in your exemplary use
of words the pain and pleasure of saying goodbye
and what you will miss. Stage 4 cancer.
Malignant melanoma. You call it your *'end time'.*
Goodbye. Goodbye.
What's so god damn good about it, anyway?

https://www.terrain.org/2020/nonfiction/what-ill-miss/

I am a Poem

I am a poem
rhyming sometimes
while painting
a melody of words.

I am a poem
with no rhyme at all
except for the
spaces left between.

I am a poem
with tales of fate
so a reader can
relate and appreciate.

I am a poem
without strict rules,
curfews
or proper manners.

I am a poem
like a wild animal
with an instinct
to survive.

I am a poem
in its birthday suit.
Naked,
without embarrassment.

I am a poem
striving for authenticity.
Displaying my truth
so others can see it.

I am a poem
looking for protection
inside the pages of a book
between the outside covers.

I am a poem
that will live on
beyond the life
of mortal man.

I am a poem.
Written with purpose
or simply a whim.
Remaining, nevertheless.

I am a poem.
Not asking for your approval.
Hoping you'll just allow
what poems do best.

Boomerang

I believe in karma.
Universe of balance.
An in and an out.
What goes up must come down.
If there's wrong, there's right.
Lies countered with truth.

Karma is benevolent justice.
Fervently fair.
One never knows how it will
deal with dubious behavior.
It just does it in its
metaphysical, tenacious way.

For every action
there's a reaction.
Serenity for every storm.
Karma constantly in motion.
Correcting the imbalance
of evil versus good for
believer and misanthrope.

Karma works
in uncanny ways.
Happens at the right time
at the right place
to the right person.
Believe in karma or not –
you're always in its jurisdiction.

Human, Being

A tree is known by its fruit; man by his deeds.
Good deeds are never lost; sowing courtesy reaps friendship,
planting kindness gathers love.

– Saint Basil of Caesarea

Pet a dog.
Give away your smile.
Realize there are
no mistakes,
just lessons.
Be a human, being.

Show kindness.
Take chances.
Realize you will
never be perfect.
Embrace your flaws and virtues.
Be a human, being.

Have a child's imagination.
Play. Be corny. Be silly.
Realize life's
too short to be
so solemnly serious.
Be a human, being.

Find friends.
Be worthy of them.
Realize it's all over
quicker than you think.
Make memories.
Be a human, being.

We share it with
every human on earth.
Realize ripples you create
are vibrations
released upon the universe.
You are a human, being.

Good for Boeing

My father worked for Boeing –
a primary player in the
military-industrial complex.
"War means jobs" was his mantra.
I believe he actually meant
"What's good for Boeing is good for me."
Which put food on the table.
Clothes on his family's back.
And money for a rainy day
in the savings and loan bank account.

Vietnam was a lousy excuse
to feed the military-industrial machine.
It was a political war
as opposed to a patriotic one.
Yet, Dad was a gung-ho hawk
in favor of the conflict's escalation.
It was good for Boeing.

He was steadfast in his conviction.
Once, on a camping trip with friends,
he debated his point-of-view
into the wee hours of the morning
with a fellow recently married
to one of the friend's daughters.
A soft-spoken, gentle long-haired hippy.
No matter what the logic of
abandoning our commitment
to an unjust war, Dad was resolute –
wrapping his heart and emotion
unconditionally in the red, white and blue.

Even when I received my selective service card
and waited for my number in the draft lottery,
it wasn't a matter for open discussion.
Some of my friends talked of fleeing to Canada
or becoming a conscientious objector.
In my father's eyes, they were all cowards.
His perspective came from a different time.
Different reasons. Different war.

My draft number was 76 in 1972.
A year before, they drafted those
with numbers less than 125. I waited.
Then the news announced the number
would be 95 for my draft year.
All I could do is wait for my induction notice
and pray to my angels to grant a miracle.
They did.
Due to the winding down of the war
and upcoming Paris peace talks,
none of the 95 draft numbers were called
for those born in 1953.
I didn't have to become a coward
and break my father's heart.

Pierre Bruneau (far left) accepts his Boeing 707 trophy for December 1957 Man of the Month. He used his bonus money to pay for his son's upcoming hernia operation.

The Mirror Reflects

I see my father in the mirror.
It's not him, it's supposed to be me.
It's 7:30 in the morning
and I see his smiling eyes
and wry grin staring back.

Even my morning groans
and nose blows
are an etched remembrance
of his odd waking sounds
comforting a child's contentment.

He is still with me – my father.
Although he has passed on,
rejoining my mother
along with the other relatives
I was so lucky to have known.

Sometimes I hear him, his voice,
coming out of my mouth,
saying something I normally would never say.
I am surprised when it happens
thinking to myself, "Hello Dad."

If I'm lucky, I don't have to apologize
for my father's content or conduct.
Or be embarrassed by the consequences.
I do my best to move on, proceeding
with the restoration of myself.

When I look in the mirror,
I observe a much older version
than what's in my mind's eye.
Perhaps that's why I spend
as little time as possible in front of it.

I accept my father's resemblance,
but not a comparison.
Ironing out his wrinkles –
the concrete
for the foundation of my personality.

The mirror is just a reflection, after all.

The Popcorn Bowl

I remember Dad's large pyrex popcorn bowl –
red on the outside, white on the inside,
with caramel-colored old maids at the bottom –
on the counter to be washed after last evening's use.
If you were lucky, he'd leave a few popped kernels
or at least some semi-popped ones
you could scoop up in the remaining salty butter.

Popcorn was a common evening treat in our home,
usually prepared after children were in bed,
supposedly asleep, supposedly deaf
to the sporadic rat-a-tat-tat of the popper –
coming to a climax as the corn lifted the glass lid
making the few final pops even louder
and hearing delicate clinks of the treat
poured into the large bowl.

Then, a pat of butter into the still-hot popper
with a sizzle – and a little shake to keep from burning,
frosting the alabaster morsels with delicious goodness.
The aroma would waft into the bedroom
and sometimes be too much to bear
to continue pretending to be asleep.
I would rise from bed, coyly ask for a drink of water
and look longingly at the full red popcorn bowl
now on my father's lap. Mother would retrieve
a plastic coffee cup from the cupboard
and put in a handful of the white fluffy goodness
before dispatching me off to bed.

Sliding back into the covers, I slowly
nibbled on my precious tidbit of a treasure
and listened to the muffled sounds
of their quiet conversation and
babble from the black & white television
while I drifted happily off to sleep.

French Kiss

Always kissed both
my mother and father
on the mouth.
Never thought it unusual.
Told it was because
my father was French.

Pierre is a French name,
that's for sure.
But one would have to
examine three or four
generations back
to find anyone fluent.

In fact, the only French
I ever heard him speak
was "Sacré bleu!"
Yet, throughout my life
I kissed Dad
straight on his lips.

Arriving home from work,
I still recall the
coarseness of his
five o'clock shadow
on my tender young skin.
Just his way to show love.

Can't remember
when I discovered
kissing one's father
was something
ordinarily
regulated to a cheek.

Of course,
I was also surprised
to find out
French kissing
had little to do
with being French.

It was a family quirk –
innocent as
it was affectionate.
On his deathbed, at 87,
I said my final goodbye
on his cold, dying lips.

Because we were French.

We Start Out as Children

Initially, we are beginners.
Learning
to eat, to talk, to walk,
to listen, to love.
At first,
the only thing we are good at
is filling our diapers.
Time goes on
and we get better
at all the traits
that help us grow into adulthood.
Filing our minds
with more grown up things
while abandoning adolescence.

As children, we played.
Used our imagination.
Were color-blind.
Culture-blind.
Sang songs out of tune
without an ounce of embarrassment.
Caught grasshoppers in a jar.

We start out as children
and as we grow older
some of that
precious childhood innocence
is replaced by matters of maturity.

In so many ways,
the world would be
much better off
if we didn't have to shed
the purity we were born with
only to wear the armor adults require
in order to survive.

Vigilante

I remember when
you were a Vigilante, Dad.
Not a real one
who would chase
undesirables out of town
and hang cattle rustlers –
but part of a square dance fraternity
who would shoot
blanks in their guns at parades,
kidnap unsuspecting onlookers
and lock them up behind bars
in the jail on top of their float.
When mother made you
the faux cowhide vest,
she made a miniature one for me.
With my Roy Rogers cap gun
I could pretend to be just like you.
Standing on top of the table –
part of the patio set you bought
from the Hispanic family down the road –
I felt big – wearing my cowhide vest
and silver sheriff's badge –
thinking how lucky I was
that you were my father
and we were both
on the same side of the law.

Bad Answers to Good Questions

Why is the sky blue?
Don't have a clue. Wish I knew.

Why is grass green?
To make brown dirt less obscene.

Why does the ocean roar?
It's better than if you heard it snore.

Why does the wind blow?
It's just the air waving hello.

Why is it dark at night?
In order for the day to have the light.

Why are there seasons?
The months probably have a reason.

Why is water so wet?
Dry water is not invented yet.

Why is there thunder?
To wake a storm from its slumber.

Why do we get old?
Our parts wear out, truth be told.

Why do we cry?
It keeps sadness from being shy.

Rest of the Story

Want to know the
rest of the story?
The part that begins
when last chapter ends.
Adventures beyond the book.

What became of Alice who
fell through the looking glass?
The release of Jim
in Huckleberry Finn –
did they sustain success?

We can only imagine.
Fill in unwritten lines.
Was Alice committed
to a sanitarium?
Did old Jim
move on to crime?

Pursuit for any story
not inside the book cover.
Are there clues from
authors' rough drafts?
Were there notes
about another?

It's left to us to visualize
what the future holds.
Not just in books but
everyday existence.
Predict tomorrow.
Watch the world unfold.

Walking the Blind Dog Through the Graveyard at Dusk

Skipper sniffs an old gravestone while we pass.
It's a landmark for the dog. He's been here before.
Dozens of others previously left their scent
yet, his nose detects his familiar flavor.
It's a compass now that his eyesight is gone.
A sense compensating for the other lost.
He remembers where he is and lets out a yip.
One of his favorite walks when he could see.
His black tail wags delight. Takes the lead.
Maneuvering past stone dominos with ease.
Guiding me through the cemetery maze
as dusk collapses into darkness,
welcoming the stars, one-by-one.
And I, without a flashlight.
Skipper knows the way home from here.
Dog duties still important
no matter the handicap.

Better a blind dog than none at all.

Joni

I wish I had known you then.
Singing your poetry so confidently –
a woman in control.
A woman expressing her wisdom,
composure, certainty.
A woman expressing her skepticism,
vulnerability, sensitivity.
Just you and me, alone together
listening to the LP –
lyrics speaking to my heart.

Perhaps, I should have abandoned school
and driven to Laurel Canyon.
Would you have been my friend?
Ten years older and so much wiser.
As a girlfriend, I didn't intend.
I'd leave that for David or Graham
or fellow Canadian Neil.
But I would have loved to know
what made you tick.
Learn what made you feel.

For the Roses is still my favorite.
Capturing the devotion
of a precocious eighteen year old
with words that shaped my life.
Listening again, forty seven years later,
it catapults me back instantly
to that fresh, frustrating, formative time
that helped craft the whole of me.

I remember you complaining on
Miles of Aisles about the audience
demanding to hear your old songs.
You said they never would ask Van Gogh
to paint another *Starry Night*.
But I can listen without your permission
as many times as I desire.
Experience my own starry night
as my soulful reflection transpires.

A German duo, Lizn Taylor, recorded a song and used my poem for the lyrics. https://soundcloud.com/edmond-bruneau/joni

Rabbit Ears

One night,
the cable went out.
Turned off the TV.
I'll fix it in the morning.

Donna said,
"When we were young,
all one had to do
was
turn a knob."

Which was true.
It was an easier,
simpler life.
Actually,
we could still do that.

Sacrifice the effortless
150 channel selection.
Abandon the ability
to record six different shows
at the same time.

We would have to
simply watch what was on.
Or listen to the radio hoping
the DJ would play
our favorite new song.

Now it involves a cable signal.
Modem. Router. Internet.
The modern version of rabbit ears,
with pieces of foil crimped onto
the antenna for better reception.

Not to mention the bother
of getting up from the couch
and changing channels on the TV.
Remote controls were a
clunky rare commodity.

Donna's right.
We live in much more
complicated times.
Lost without our phone
in our pocket or purse.

If our devices
won't connect to a signal
or the cable ceases to work,
we go into a full-on panic
as if one of our limbs were removed.

Modern technology
has given us
many wonderful conveniences –
unfortunately while
increasing our dependency.

And we still want more.
The latest. The fastest.
The most features.
If we could only get
next year's model today.

There are times I wouldn't mind
fussing with rabbit ears
to get a clearer picture.
Turning one knob and simply
seeing things in black and white.

Horse Latitudes

Full sail.
Cast upon waters.
Headed for destination
unknown.
Moving forward.
To discovery.
To new adventure.
To enrich
through experience.

But alas,
we come upon
horse latitudes.
With no wind
to fill our sails.
Or fish
to feed our souls.
Dead in the water
until a new breeze blows.

It's out of our hands
now.
Stuck in the
Calms of Cancer.
At the mercy
of nature
and circulation
of atmosphere.
We wait.

And set.
Until the wind blows.
Until the wind blows.
Until the wind blows.

Tulip Festival

Annual pilgrimage, weather dependent.
At worst, we only saw yellow daffodils.
At best, chromatic retina refreshment.
My favorite part –
traipsing through bulb gardens,
lost in fields of color abandon –
kaleidoscope kismet.
The worst part –
enduring your hillbilly kinfolk.

When your next older sister died,
we began to attend in her honor.
Even then,
the visits seemed more forced,
dredging up her memories
instead of commemorating them.
We did it 'til
you could no longer –
when your short bloom, like tulips,
began to fade.

Tried visiting once again
in my second life –
and although the flowers
were probably as beautiful,
it unearthed remembrance
which only one of us could relate.
Best to make new memories
without ghosts
or ethereal haunts –
and not return where
spirits and sadness sojourn.

Making the Grade

On the right track.
Get out of the rain.
Pray light at tunnel end
is not a coming train.

Do for yourself –
not for accolade.
Opportunity knocks.
The rest is fate.

Heartache happens.
Feelings fade.
Resist temptation –
be it jezebel or jade.

Engage, not enrage.
It's not a debate.
Know the meaning of
façade and charade.

All that shines isn't gold.
Haste does make waste.
Read between the lines
before they're all erased.

Head above water.
Made in the shade.
Right side of the grass.
Making the grade.

I Can Live with You

I can live with you.
I can love with you.
Collaborate our joys and fears
and fill my life with you.
Engage in ordinary moments
and make it memorable just the same.
Indeed, I can live with you
sharing pleasures and the pain.

I can live with you
into the great unknown.
Tomorrow predicted
but not assured.
I can love with you.
Explore uncharted terrain.
Have adventures for dessert.

For no matter
what we gain or lose
we have each other, you and me.
Even as we become antique.
Grow old, feeble and frail.
I can live with you.
I can love with you.
My devotion will not fail.

I can live with you.
I can love with you
as long as it sustains.
As long as your hand's in mine
and sunsets still remain.

Uncle Don

The last time I saw my Uncle Don
he couldn't speak.
Cruel Mad Cow Disease
robbed him of that ability.

I refuse to remember him that way.
In a hospital bed, helpless.
Yet, memories do resurface.

As a boy, I recall
getting a stuffed dog toy
made from llama fur
he brought home
from his Navy
Icebreaker tour.

Or, when he would draw
Disney characters to color,
especially Donald Duck.
And gave me a lesson
on how to do it myself.

I think he was happiest
when he used his
artistic temperament
upholstering furniture.

And his laugh –
a contagious howl
that infected the room.
God, I wish I could hear it again.

Be it summer and sultry
or winter and wind –
any day was the perfect day
to find a spot for fishing.

We all ate the same beef
from Grandfather's Herefords –
twenty years without harm.
Why was he chosen
to take the bullet?
I'm pretty sure
I saw a smile appear on his face
when I shared some moments
we had together,
which I still hold dear.

A gentle, left-handed,
artistic fishing enthusiast
who always had time
for his nephew.
Until this rare disease
happened upon him.

Mad Cow.

Wow.

The Magician

In the blink of an eye
he made things vanish.
They were here
and then were gone.
Where did they go
when they disappeared?
Vanquished to a void
in the great beyond?

That's the magician's secret.
He alone knows where.
Pockets, open and empty.
His hands completely bare.
The beauty of the mystery
is not where it all went.
Or how the illusion tricked us
without our own consent.

No, the joy is in the magic.
Sleight of hand, misdirection.
The skill of making us believe –
fall for the misconception.
Don't look for illumination.
Or for any conspicuous clue.
Marvel at the bewitchment –
and how it happened to you.

Michelangelo Sanitized

Don't put a
fig leaf on David
and hide the artist's truth.
Or cover up
those voluptuous nudes
and make the
Renaissance uncouth.
Art is a vision –
a personal, social,
sometimes controversial
point-of-view.
It speaks from its creator.
And perhaps to me and you.
Is there guilt by association?
Only if you allow.
We are judged by what
we sculpt each day –
including raising our brow.

White Bread

Wholesome, they told us.
Enriched for your health.
Builds strong bodies 12 ways.
Wonder which was the twelfth?

Highly processed flour.
Additives for good measure.
Lack of bran and germ
made it lesser, not better.

Every childhood sandwich
from store-bought white loaf.
Mothers thought nutritious.
Essential for our growth.

Misguided for so long.
Vitamin deficiencies. Malnutrition.
Antidote for its poison –
added iron, thiamin, niacin.

Kids disliked brown bread.
100 percent whole wheat.
Had fiber. Texture. Taste.
Nothing we wanted to eat.

Times have changed.
Nourishment priority.
Whole wheat popularity
for population majority.

Kool-aid. Jello salad.
Candy cigarettes.
Gone the way of the TV tray.
And mothers' fare regrets.

Change

Today, I upgraded my
computer operating system
in order to extend usefulness
for other software that wouldn't
function well any longer.
I didn't want to. I had to. Forced to.
Probably by a young software developer
who does not realize that, at my age,
I think of change as a choice,
not a requirement.

In the computer world,
everything is linked together.
Everything works better
if it's newer and improved
with more features and capabilities.
Quicker. More efficient.
Until it reaches a point
when the computer is too old
to be upgraded any longer.
It no longer functions as it should –
so discard and replace it
with a spanking new model.

Personally, I don't want to be replaced
with a quicker, smarter, faster version.
I embrace the reality that my brain
isn't quite as keen as it used to be.
It takes me longer to think of
an answer to a trivia question.
Even though I may know it,
a newer, more modern human
likely will beat me to the punch.
Wisdom and experience
can't be downloaded for immediate access.
It has to be accumulated the old fashioned way.
As I age and become surrounded
by better, smarter, faster versions –
I'm content with my aging operating system,
positioning myself as a valuable antique –
cherished and treasured
as an oddity from another time.

Picnic Nitpick

Picnics were different
in my childhood.
Portable bbq grill,
laden with charcoal
and lighter fluid,
exploding with a match
thrown five feet away
to avoid hair singe.

Kool-aid in waxy paper cups.
Watermelon with seeds.
Hotdogs were just hotdogs
that shrunk when cooked.
If too hungry to wait,
kids would eat them raw.
Toppings were yellow mustard,
ketchup and sweet relish
on bleached white buns.

Lime green Jello.
Sometimes with bananas.
Or carrot shavings.
Potato salad. Potato chips. Celery.
If you didn't like it,
the solution was simple.
Go hungry.
Everyone ate
the same thing.

Desserts were often
cupcakes and twinkies.
Once in a while
you'd get a Dixie Cup with
vanilla ice cream on one side,
orange sherbet on the other.
Eaten with a flat wooden spoon.
Or a popsicle, orange or red,
guaranteed to drip on your shirt.

If swimming nearby, it meant
waiting an hour after eating.
A family member
became the official timer,
who got used to repeatedly
saying to children, "Not yet."
Teeter-totters in every park.
Self-powered merry-go-rounds.

Fond memories
of those past picnics.
Before safety concerns demanded
lighter fluid less volatile.
Teeter-totters and metal
merry-go-rounds eliminated.
Vegan preferences and
gluten allergies making
traditional menus difficult.

If we could go back in time.
Unravel all the changes –
kids could experience
how it feels
to slide down a hot metal slide
in the heat of the day.
Spit out watermelon seeds
like a machine gun.
Eat hotdogs 'til full.

Kids now given a Lunchable®,
washing it down with a
Capri Sun® juice pouch.
Playground equipment
made of plastic.
Parents possessed by their phones,
sipping their Starbucks® –
as if they wish they were
anyplace but there.

Bluenose

I remember when it happened.
Cold winter day on the playground.
He took one look at me and said,
"Your nose is turning a little blue."
From then on, a new nickname.

Bluenose Bruneau.
Hopscotch kids thought it hilarious.
Bluenose stuck like glue.
Not sociable as "Smitty"
or endearing as "Dino."

Didn't know at the time
it meant priggish or hoity-toity.
Confused it with brownnose
which was a shitty nickname, too.
Hated it. Felt belittled.

I think about the person who
created that cruel characterization.
Became the Bluenose promoter.
Laughs and snickers at my expense.
Called himself my friend.

Just endured it.
Smiled as if I was
in on the joke.
Never once indicated
it pissed me off.

Learned later in life
that putting people down
is a method to feel superior.
Wants others to like him better.
Motivated by low self-esteem.

Sadistic thing to do
to a seven year old boy.
Perhaps a bloody red nose
would have nipped it in the bud.
Bluenose will never know.

Pee Chee

It wasn't until junior high
when I was introduced to the Pee Chee.
It was, at the time, an inexpensive folder
to keep papers and handouts together
for each different class.
Inside, its flaps revealed
conversion tables, multiplication tables
and tables of measurement
which hardly ever came in handy.
Back when it was introduced in 1943,
the paper card stock was peach colored,
immortalizing its funny name in
our secondary education DNA.
Corny sports illustrations
braving the Pee Chee cover
were easily defaced,
often with scurrilous doodles
and thought balloons.
Like so many things in
today's modernness,
the sturdy, yellow
all season portfolio
has been erased
from current vocabulary –
convicted and sentenced
to remain a part of
baby boomer nostalgia –
allowing us an outlet
for artistic creativity
during a tedious
science lecture.

A period of time when
life was *"peachy keen"*.

Mother Goosed

Jack and Jill went to Brazil
to each become transgender.
Jack's now Jill, and waited until
Jill became Jack thereafter.

Jack Sprat had no facts.
His wife was just plain mean.
Both complained the election stolen
by a tampered voting machine.

Georgy Porgy was a bad guy.
Kissed the girls and made them cry.
Didn't stand for such torment.
Sued him for sexual harassment.

Baa, baa, black sheep
why are you so rightful?
If it's restitution you seek,
today we're all remorseful.
What our great great grandfathers did
obviously was a shame.
Too many generations passed
to satisfy such a claim.

Bye, baby bunting
Father is disgusting.
Mother's gone a-sulking.
Sister's simply insulting.
Brother's gone looking for kin
to take poor baby bunting in.

Little Miss Muffet
thought she could rough it
but conditions became her dismay.
Though she was a fighter
there was no one to guide her.
Died in complete disarray.

Just Desserts

The three little kittens, they lost their mittens,
And they began to cry,
"Oh, mother dear, we sadly fear,
That we have lost our mittens."
"What! Lost your mittens, you naughty kittens!
Then you shall have no pie."
"Meow, meow, meow."
"Then you shall have no pie."

This Mother Goose poem
worried me as a child.

First, these honest kittens
explain to their mom
their mittens are perhaps lost.
They're feeling terrible about it.
Just as I would
if I had lost my own mittens.
Confession may be
good for the soul –
but what horrible mother
shows no compassion
for the little ones and
screams how naughty they have been?
Mittens are difficult to keep
on paws in the first place.
Icing on the punishment cake
is no pie. *No pie!!*
Actions have consequences
but restricting the little furballs
from their favorite pastry
seems cruel and unusual.
If I lost *my* mittens,
I would tie them to my wrists next time.
A clean and simple solution
showing ingenuity and problem solving.
Certainly, I hope my discipline
more mellow than
forever forbidding pie.
Maybe a time out
like little Jack Horner.
He was able to have pie
WHILE he was in the corner.
Better reprimand for one's "just desserts".

The Variations

I don't recall how we got the gig
at the Rebekah Lodge in downtown Redmond
but I think my grandmother
had something to do with it.
It was an old building with wooden floors
and served as a dance hall in the past.
We set up for our musical debut
on the small stage in one of the corners –
my red sparkle Slingerland drum set
and the microphones and amplifiers.
Four thirteen/fourteen year-old boys
ready to showcase our musical talents
for the private party who rented the room.
My mother had sewn us costumes –
long sleeve pullover shirts with nehru collars
in bright gold glitter material.
A sight to behold, I'm sure.
We began playing at 8pm, as scheduled,
beginning with the *"House of the Rising Sun"*
and segueing into the Beatles' *"Yesterday"*
and *"Ticket to Ride."* As the band played on,
we began to venture into
some of our more energetic numbers
like *"Wipe Out"* and *"Gloria."*
That's when I began to notice
the lovely attire my mother had
painstakingly prepared for us
DID NOT BREATHE.
We were all sweating profusely,
drenching the garments.
By the time we rocked into Hendrix's
"Purple Haze," the lead guitarist and
bass player already stripped to a t-shirt.
Since my mother had worked so hard on them,
I was last to shed the sodden shirt.
The Variations played at other venues,
but sans the special attire.
Mine hung in the closet for years.

I couldn't throw it away.

Tami

She chirps like a bird
rolling her “r’s”
requesting immediate
gratification
from the petting factory.
She snuggles up on my lap
tips the bill of my cap
and gives me ear kisses.
Then settles down a bit
still in full purr
licks my hand like lapping milk
with an occasional love bite.
She is a hot water bottle
soothing my ailments,
providing me calm
better than
any other medicine.
Finally, the purring stops
and she stretches out full length –
front paws forward,
back feet behind
then curling
into a black and white
cinnamon roll
of contentment.

Love's Reflection

You might admire.
You might aspire.
You might worship
the ground walked upon
with devotion and desire.
You might like.
You might cherish.
Perhaps even revere.
But you cannot love
until you love yourself.
Let's make that very clear.

You're the person whom you're with
every moment, twenty-four/seven.
How can you love another when
your own love lacks affection?

Love your quirks; bad habits.
Love your imperfections.
Love your faults
same as your finer points.
Abandon your own dejection.

Then, and only then
can you love someone else the same.
Embrace the quirks and weirdness
of another, unashamed.
Love isn't about picking and choosing
just the qualities you desire.
Love is the whole enchilada.
Not a portion, but the entire.

Gift of Today

Every day, another gift –
valuable as a golden goose.
Open after you've woken.
Use however you choose.

Gift of health. Gift of wealth –
no meaning without today.
Past is gone and can't respond.
Future is a day away.

Present is now –
this moment and the next.
Forward through the orchard.
Fruit gathered as you progress.

Easy to take for granted,
this existence we chisel.
What you do is up to you.
Genuine or superficial.

Today is a special gift
only if you participate.
Arrive alive, honey and hive –
the flipside, not so great...

Bingo

Before 1971,
bingo was a crime
in Washington State.

Churches illegally held
fundraising bingo events
underground.
Quietly, in a whisper,
for fear of gaining
the authority's attention.

Threat of fines, penalties
and being shut down
kept church bingo
hidden as possible.
When discovered,
parishioners ashamed.

One would have thought
the government
was going after the mob
for heaven's sake.
Eleven years later,
Washington State
had its own lottery.

If the state decides
money can be made,
what was once illegal
becomes right as rain.

Devil's weed.
Assassin of youth.
Reefer madness.
Gateway drug
surely leading
to heroin.

Half century ago,
a one joint bust
could yield
ten years of jail time.

In 2020,
sanctioned cannabis stores
boosted Washington State revenue
by $474 million dollars –
nearly double the
annual income versus
liquor and beer taxes.

The gold of pot
is not
at the end of the rainbow,
but filling state coffers, instead.

Bingo.

The Last Thing

The last thing I'd want to do
is walk a tightrope.
Without a net.
Something I would regret.

The last thing I'd want to do
is wash skyscraper windows.
It would be a pain
to clean the panes.

The last thing I'd want to do
is hazmat dive in a sewer –
obtaining an education
in defecation.

The last thing I'd want to do
is be an animal masturbator
procuring sperm samples.
I'm sure there's other examples.

The last thing I'd want to do
is kill another human being.
With a gun. A knife. A car.
Would be forever scarred.

The last thing I'd want to do
is die.
One day I will. Adieu.
The absolute last thing I do.

What's Your Name Again?

When we introduced ourselves
you told me your name.
Moments later, it was gone.
Was it Mike or Mick
or Jim or John?
I wish I could remember.
Maybe I'll just listen in –
let someone else
say it again.
My forgetfulness
surrenders.

They say if you
associate names
with something
they resemble,
it helps with the memory –
improves mediocre mental.
Bruce looks like a mongoose.
Lana slim like a banana.
Paul because he is so tall.
Louise from Louisiana.
Fred has an enormous head.
Charlie's such a smarty.
Ruby's hair scarlet red.
Harry – that's self-explanatory.

Next time you are introduced
make this trick your friend.
If it works, you'll never have to ask
"What's your name again?"

Freedom from Fear

That was the image
burned into his brain.
A perfect planet
of love, safety and protection.
Now he's the grownup
and the world is far from fine.

His freedom from fear
translated into his gun collection.
One shotgun, one semiauto,
and four pistols.
High caliber security.
Peace by his definition.

He watched the evening news.
With astonishment. With anger.
Feeding his depressive nature
with sadness of the stories.
Seeing his
freedom from fear disappear.

The call came in to 9-1-1,
claiming the world had gone mad.
He knew the Rockwell image
no longer existed.
So many one-parent homes.
Children taking themselves to bed.

One of the pistol barrels
found a way into his mouth.
Cops knocking on the front door,
wanting inside.
Battering ram
breaking the door down.

Only took one
discharge of the weapon.
An escape in his time machine –
where kids say their prayers
and fall fast asleep under parental watch –
sheltered from life's stark realities.

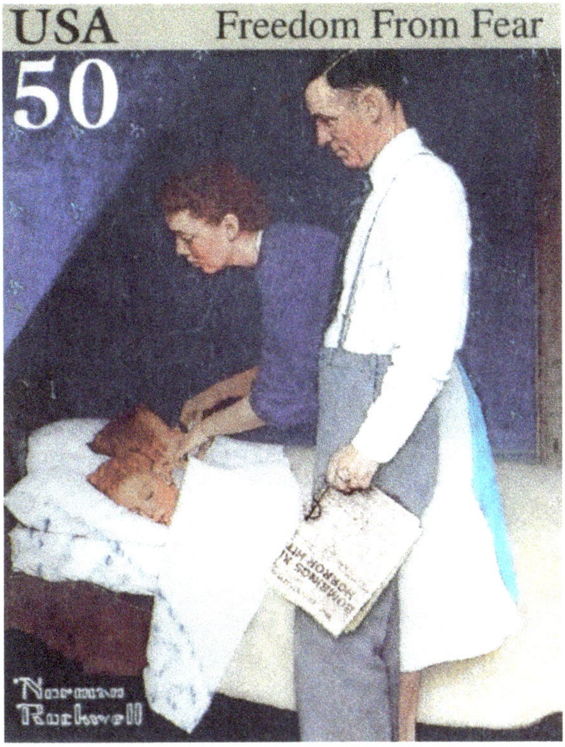
USA
Freedom From Fear
50
Norman
Rockwell

*Norman Rockwell painted a picture of ideality –
Mom and Dad lovingly tucking two young gingers into bed,
even when the newspaper in father's hand reveals
a headline of bombing and horror.*

Freedom From Want
USA
50
Norman
Rockwell

Lost Tradition

I'm reminded of the iconic
Norman Rockwell painting
of a family celebrating Thanksgiving –
such joy and exuberance
surrounding the turkey as
it's set down on the dinner table.

Rockwell's portrait,
Freedom from Want
is nostalgically wonderful
and so blatantly unrealistic
reflecting our modern age.

Mother in her apron,
father in suit and tie.
Patriarch at the head of the table
and the smiling family engaged
in fun, lively conversations.
Without television football
blaring in the background.
Uninterrupted by cell phone calls,
searches and texts.
Or polarizing political discussions.
Or concerns
whether or not the food is
organic, GMO, gluten free
or vegan.

Many have lost such a tradition
in favor of succumbing to the
various distractions surrounding us.
I long for the simplicity
of a home cooked feast
shared by people we love
with manners, respect,
kindness and gratefulness.

Such a Thanksgiving,
no matter what the era,
is truly a blessing.

A Salamander Tale

She woke from a dream
losing her tail
with great regret.
Fortunate she was a salamander
where appendages
do grow back.

Even though
it was just a dream
it was a pleasant one at that.
The thought a lung
now gone from her
could return again, perhaps.

But we are not lizards,
nor starfish or lobster.
Wounds do not grow back.
We must transform
ourselves instead –
reconcile and adapt.

No matter the trauma,
exhaustion or pain –
be it heartbreak,
disease, distress or distrain.
We can't replace it as it was.
It's a chance to start fresh again.

Pan Dora

Just an email –
with attachment.
From someone
I do not know.
First name, Pan.
Last name, Dora.
Curiosity satisfied
with a quick click.

But wait.
Why do I want
to unleash
uncertainly?
Could be a worm.
A shanghai.
A pirate promise
of glitter gold.

Used to take
extensive exploration
to discover
her trunk of
non-innocence.
Now she comes to you.
In an email.
Or fake Facebook friend.

With lure.
Sex, money, grandeur.
Subconscious seductress.
She has you alone.
No one to prevent you
from biting the hook –
Except one's own decision
to dance with Delilah.

Yes, Pan Dora.
You invade my domain.
You hold the key
to things I shouldn't see.
And things
I cannot unsee.
Today, you stay buried.
Unopened. Trashed.

But there's always tomorrow.
I may be more careless.
Or the cat might
walk on my keyboard.
I will attempt to prevent you
seducing me with temptation.
Internet transcendence makes
it all so damn easy to succumb.

Summer Gone

I miss the sunny morning warm glow
of our outdoor breakfast on the patio.
You said
this might be our last day
in shorts, without coats,
and I didn't believe you.
It's too soon for summer to leave –
abandoning its duty. Its obligation.
Its welcome presence as our seasonal guest.
But you were right.
The crispness of autumn blew in
and with it, the demise of
those lofty summer mornings.
Like our hummingbirds on
one sad summer day –
when we noticed
we no longer had winged joy
drinking from our feeders.
Summer, too, has moved on,
packed its knapsack and headed south –
bringing breakfast back indoors
and leaving harmonious memories
in the dust of its disregard.

Squirreling Away

Beguiled by autumn squirrel stockpilers
scampering about in heedful urgency
makes me concerned they know
something we don't about winter approaching.
It's been cooler this fall
by an average of ten degrees
and I fear the word
one only whispers –
"snow"–
may be just around the corner.
We already turned our home's heat on
a month earlier than last year.
And chances are, all the leaves
will drop before Halloween.
Like the squirrels,
Donna has already put the garden away
and has begun to pile pine needles
for plants she hopes to winter over.
I recently gave the snowblower
a tune-up and annual oil change.
I hope there's time
to take in the hoses and
trim down the roses
before the killing frost.
It's all too soon to give up hope
for a radiant Indian summer.
Menopausal Mother Nature
will do what she wants,
when she wants,
leaving us powerless
to her whim.
We can only get a hint
watching the squirrels gather it in.

Magnajector©

Began asking Santa
for a Magnajector©
when I was five.
Sears Toy Catalog page
damaged from
constant drooling.

Imagine.
Any image you want
projected four feet wide.
Dreamt of doing a
Sunday comic show
for the cousins.

Our own masterpieces
in pencil and Crayola
enlarged on the wall
like a movie theater.
My list was a short one,
with Magnajector© on top.

Don't know why Santa
forgot it that Christmas.
Or the following one.
Perhaps my parents
found the toy exorbitant.
Thought I was "too young."

Two years of disappointment.
My incessant campaign
finally wore them down.
There it was, under the tree,
in all its bakelite glory.
Christmas dream fulfilled.

Hours of entertainment.
Magazines. Family photos.
Larger than life. High tech
in our analog world of
rotary dial phone and
black and white TV.

One day I broke the mirror –
relentless use, I suppose.
Still could use it, even with
large crack in projection.
First time I felt guilt and sadness
over a fractured favorite treasure.

Carefully put it away
in its cardboard "suitcase."
Placed on the bedroom shelf –
where it would sit until
zeal overcame shame
to try again, scar and all.

Magnajector®
Patented
PROJECTS
A 4" PICTURE
TO FOUR FEET WIDE
IN ACTUAL COLOR!
(no slides, no films required.)
FUN!
EDUCATIONAL!
ALL AGES!
HANDY LUGGAGE-TYPE CARRYING CASE!
PATENTED
USES STANDARD HOUSEHOLD LIGHT BULB!
BIG TV PROMOTION!
$7.95 SUGGESTED RETAIL
ASK ABOUT SHOPPER-STOPPER DISPLAY
MAGNAJECTOR, destined for one of the biggest TV pushes in toy selling history! This handsome opaque projector enlarges any illustrated material up to 4 feet wide. No films or negatives required! Magazines, comics, newspapers, snapshots, coloring book figures—all are projected clearly in full color or black and white for endless hours of entertainment. Patented functional design in gleaming ebony black. Insulated socket housing takes ordinary household light bulb. Adjustable twin lenses. Approved by Underwriters' Laboratories, Inc. Overall dimensions: 12" long x 8" high x 4½" wide. Six to shipper. Wt. 14 lbs.
RAINBOW CRAFTS, INC.
CINCINNATI 12, OHIO

Sweet Tooth Savings Plan

Before I had any money to save,
my sister and I
devised an insidious plan
to keep us in candy all year long.
It began on Halloween,
going door to door
for treats instead of tricks.
At home, we'd examine our riches –
sort them by type and size
and hide them away
in an old shoe box
safely stored in our dresser drawers.

The challenge then
was not to eat all the treasure
until Christmas,
when we'd hit the motherlode
and again rejoice in
our newly acquired wealth.
We each had our own methods
not to be without.
It was a challenge. A competition.
Enjoying one's candy
slow enough – wisely enough –
to make it to the next sugar depot.

From Christmas,
it was Valentine's Day
when my punctual father
would always be late
coming home from work that afternoon –
presenting us with small versions
of the large heart he'd given mom.

Then Easter –
the torture being
if it was early or late
that particular year.
The chocolate rabbit
and marshmallow chicks
all found lodging in
the shoe box in the drawer.

Then, the six month drought.
No candy holidays
until the following Halloween.
That's when the going got tough
and the weak ate candy.
Sometimes, I misered a few pieces away
from Halloween and Christmas
to supplement the Easter haul
and provide additional rations
for the long scarcity ahead.

By October, I was down to
chewing gum and jelly beans.
But I knew, come Halloween,
fate would again provide fortune
and we'd be back in the
confection of plenty
once again.

Trybaby

Try – one of those words
created to make failure
more palatable.
It shouldn't exist.
No one ever says they *"tried"*
completing a successful endeavor.
"At least I tried" whines
when attempts miss the mark.

It's like a way station
between excuse and regret.
A 'Get out of Jail' free card
when things don't go right.
The warm feeling a toddler gets
peeing in its diaper.
Failure is a crappy thing
that happens to everyone.

Simply choose to do
or do not. There is no try.
Just as there's no middle ground
between winning and losing.
Saying you *"tried"*
means proudly bringing home
a participation trophy
to put on your mantle.

If you don't achieve
the first time,
buck up and
move ahead.
Another direction.
A different tack.
Many solutions apply
to a single problem.

Or dismiss your attempt.
Cut your losses.
Throw in the towel.
Abandon ship.
Just, please, don't deliver
the lame rationalization
that *"you tried."*
It's the worst kind of self-talk.

Don't be a trybaby.

"She knows there's no success like failure
And that failure's no success at all."
– excerpt from the Bob Dylan song,
Love Minus Zero/No Limit

Pardon Me

Pardon me
if I look ahead
rather than behind.

Pardon me
If I use my eyes
instead of being blind.

Pardon me
if I use my brain
and think instead of follow.

Pardon me
if I don't make up stories
way too hard to swallow.

Pardon me
if I don't fit
exactly in your mold.

Pardon me
if I choose to be
warm instead of cold.

Pardon me
if I desire
appreciation versus envy.

Pardon me
if I prefer
paltry over plenty.

Pardon me
if I offend or
annoy you in any way.

I live my life
to please myself,
not you – and that's ok.

Early Bird

He went to work half an hour early.
Not just once in a while. Always.
It was one of his quirks –
not just being on time
but with plenty of padding as well.
He was never late.

Unless he was sick.
Or if a rare snow day prevented
a safe commute –
he'd play hooky
and sled with the kids.

It was part of his character
etched deep into his psyche.
Reliable. Steadfast. Punctual.
A man of his word.
Someone you could always count on.

They say the early bird gets the worm.
I'm not sure how that applied to him.
But he did bring home the bacon,
providing for his family in the way he knew how.
Never jeopardizing his job by being tardy.

He is gone now –
but the day he left us
I imagined him arriving at the pearly gates
half an hour earlier than all the others,
first in line for his halo and his wings.

Dog is God Spelled Backwards

I will not abandon you
if you have a bad day.
I will come when you call
and try not to disobey.
I will greet you with open heart
both tomorrow and today.
I will be here for you –
avoid being in the way.

My loyalty is beyond reproach.
My dedication without question.
My eagerness to please is obvious.
My love needs no suppression.
Please don't see me as needy ¬–
I would have to take exception.
Persistence is my existence.
Devotion, my obsession.

I am a dog. Your dog. Your pet.
Ever since I remember.
Faithful as the day is long.
My bond. My duty. My center.
Greet you when you come home
from January to December.
Eternal flame, warm and glowing –
until my own extinguished embers.

Goldie

I want to write a couplet about two people I know –
a couple who don't worry about being apropos.

Chicken named *"Goldie,"* their choice of a house pet –
an odd choice for sure - something you won't forget.

Goldie's favorite time is to sit and watch TV –
something quite unusual, that I guarantee.

She likes the news, but especially the soaps –
one about farming is more than she could hope.

If a show's too boring, she simply falls asleep –
cuddled in her master's arms, her evening then complete.

People normally choose a fish, a dog or cat –
nothing's like a chicken on one's lap, that's a fact.

Guests may smile or laugh or even give a gander –
the fella not welcome is good ole Colonel Sanders.

photo by Donna Lange

Goldie and friends inside the living room

Cat Alas

Ugly news from the Vet today.
Cancer. Sixteen-year-old cat.
Little hope for a cure.
Could choose a costly operation
that might whip it back to shape.
Or not.

Chances are,
disease has spread.
No one knows
how extensive surgery will be.
Or how quickly recovery occurs.
Decision is, for now, to watch.

One of those mammoth decisions
pet owners must make.
At sixteen years –
already last cat standing
over all the others in his tribe.
Accomplishment, nothing to sneeze at.

Still lifts our spirits with cat charm.
Doesn't seem to be in pain.
Loves the arch of a back scratched.
Even if the surgeon is successful
would the same cat return?
Anesthesia risky at such an elder age.

We weigh the considerations.
Give extra love now.
Balance the expense
with realistic expectations.
Which action delivers
the best quality of life?

Wish we could ask the cat
which road it preferred.
Surgery for longer life
accompanied with
extra pain and rehabilitation.
Or riding it out with us, together.

Pelicans in the Pond

Believe.
Majestic creatures
fly high in heavenly
blue panorama.
Circle downward spiral
into elegant
water landing.

Why now –
desiring our pond
instead of other
abundant options?
It's a drought.
Rich with fish.
Tasting what remains.

Rare visit from
unfamiliar flock.
Spirits lifted from
wing shadows
in motion.
Here for a purpose –
be it theirs or ours.

Or both.
In the animal world
one feeds another.
Emotional feast
from feathered angels
fills both
heart and soul.

The Meaning of Life

Why are we here?
Is there a plan?
Is there a reason I was born?
Is it something I can understand?

Am I supposed to help others?
Become wiser as I grow?
Am I just a part in a big machine?
Are there things I need to know?

Have I lived a life before?
Am I better than I was?
Will I have to come back again
if I do as the good book says?

It indeed is a mystery.
The mortality of it all.
The passing of our loved ones
fate fails to forestall.

The meaning of life.
The meaning of death.
Magic of a heartbeat.
Bewitchment of breath.

Perhaps it's not to reason why.
Or question our existence.
Like every other living thing
being here in its essence.

I hope there is a purpose.
I hope I play a part.
I'm thankful for the gift of days
before I disembark.

One day we will know.
Or maybe, we will not.
What matters is to live life now.
We may only get one shot.

Love is Blind

Can't see you
but feel you.
Warm soft touch
I love so much.

Can't see you
but smell you.
Your fragrance –
alluring incense.

Can't see you
but taste you.
Savoring bliss –
your sweet kiss.

Can't see you
but hear you.
Gentle intonation –
audio elation.

Can't see you
but want you.
Sharing my heart –
the important part.

I see you
without my eyes.
Reading with braille –
Living my fairytale.

Be Still

Be still.
Just for five minutes.
No mindless chatter.
No finger tapper.

Be still.
Observe.
Listen.
Let the world talk to you.

Be still.
Notice what others
call noise
is actually music.

Be still.
You can pick up
where you left off
in a few moments.

Be still.
Like a child
experiencing
the first time.

Be still.
Audience
instead of actor.
Witness the play unfold.

Be still.
Sniff the subtilely
of fragrances
fetching long, lost memories.

Be still.
Contemplate
what today's
chapter reveals.

Be still.
Discover detail
often overlooked as a blur
when we're always in motion.

Be still.
Steal something away
from quiet
examination.

Be still.
Until you laugh.
Or cry. Or gasp
in astonishment.

Be still.
Until you decide
to crawl back
into your cocoon
and resume the
numb normalcy
of daily life.

Be still.
The real world
magically appears
when you open
your eyes, nose and ears.

Just be still.

Lost Art of a Letter

Nearly extinct now –
replaced by the
instant gratification of texting
and electronically delivered email.
A handwritten letter –
a window into the writer's soul.

Writing a letter took time.
Thought. Penmanship. Purpose.
Composition.
All the while, etched with emotion,
genuine authenticity
and personal truth.

Receiving a letter
meant that someone cared
enough to put pen to paper
and write out thoughts
exclusively for you.
Then purchased a stamp for it.

No, it wasn't instant.
Delivery took days, sometimes weeks.
When it arrived,
there was a sense of anticipation
to read what was written
and savor the sentimentality.

Today, a letter is an old jalopy
in the slow lane on the freeway –
horns honking at the annoyance.
Antiquated and putting along.
Deteriorating in
our collective consciousness.

Anger

They say anger
is a form of madness.
Like a cartoon –
I imagine smoke
billowing out my ears
with my
temper seething.
My patience paralyzed.
My humor disgustingly dingy.

Who is this stranger?
Shouting. Screaming.
Exasperated.
Abandoning caring
and compassion.
In a mirror,
I wouldn't know him.

Yet, it is part of me.
Not a part I like.
But a side that
illustrates
the opposite of
my pinnacle behavior.

Unwelcome,
this rowdy visitor.
Who I beg to leave
when his actions are so foreign.
Please don't stay,
just go away
and let my love shine again.

Carving Santa

Michelangelo once explained
his work was already complete
before he even began.
He then would chisel away the stone
that wasn't part of the sculpture.
I figure that's how my mother
carved Santas
over all those years.

One Christmas, out of the blue,
my mother gave me a carved
wooden Santa Claus figure
she had created herself,
meticulously painted,
signed and dated.
Like the pine needle basket
she once wove, her talent
came out of nowhere,
without any formal art training.
It was something she wanted to do,
so she did it.

I later discovered she had carved
an identical one for my sister.
And for the next sixteen years,
she ushered in a new family tradition –
carving a new, distinctly different Santa
as her annual Christmas present
for both my sister and me.

Even as arthritis made the task
slower and painful to complete,
our new Santas always arrived at Christmas,
adding to our growing collection –
a token of a mother's enduring love.

When were told her crippled hands
could no longer chip away to the Santa inside,
it meant the end of this wonderful tradition.
The first year without a new Santa
was a somber one.
A symbol of her deteriorating mortality.

Now that she's gone,
the carved Santas are
more precious than ever –
a reminder of my mother's
incredible natural artistic talent
and her devoted, loving warmth.
The Santas she revealed
from an ordinary block of wood
live on in our holiday home
and in my eternal heart.

photo by Donna Lange

A sample of six of the Santas my mother meticulously carved

Rain

Rain seems to
amplify the emptiness.
Nightfall streetlights
make the scene
all more dreary –
changing color's palette,
into black and white noir.

A tavern on the corner ¬–
haven for the lost,
the longing, the lonely.
Fighting depression
by the glassful.
Peering outside
through dripping wet windows.

For time being,
it's a place to pretend.
A place to hide from inevitables.
A place to escape
from one's haunting soul.
A place
to get out of the rain.

Emergency Hypocrisy

You falsely cried "wolf"
far too many times
to believe you now.
There's a pattern, here –
for me as well.

My sensitive side
sucked into the drama –
attempting to see the world
through your subjective lens –
still offering guidance and hope.

Wolf,
disguised in sheep clothing.
Pulling the wool
over my eyes, once again.
Street smarts forsaken.

It is I, requiring restraint.
Discipline.
Not running to the door
every time you knock
or lend an ear to your tales of woe.

My hypocrisy –
enabling your lip service
while you continue to pick the scab.
Your wolves and wounds –
now out in the cold, where they belong.

Two Wrongs

Two wrongs don't make a right,
but three rights make a left.
Two rights don't make a wrong,
unless simply done in jest.

Look before you leap –
haste makes waste for free.
There are none so blind
as those who will not see.

Don't bite the hand that feeds you,
or the foot that gives you drink.
It's a good way to diet, I suppose,
yet, you'll probably end up extinct.

If you snooze, you lose.
Does it mean never falling asleep?
Shuteye is its own reward
with the pleasure of counting sheep.

Better safe than sorry.
Better happy than sad.
Choose the road less traveled
unless the potholes look too bad.

Every dog has its day.
Felines have nine lives.
Barking dogs seldom bite,
but they often terrorize.

Never turn your back on your face.
Nothing difficult is ever easy.
If it ain't broke, don't fix it –
unless, of course, you are Houdini.

A friend in need is a friend, indeed.
Even by hook or by crook.
Beggars can't be choosers, true,
but it's a lousy place to look.

Irish You Were Here

My four leaf clover.
My pot of gold.
My lady luck.
My heart on hold.

This day of green –
simply not the same
without your presence
fondly fanning my flame.

If I found a leprechaun,
I'd ask just one wish –
you here, with me –
instead of being missed.

Curse corned beef
and its cabbage compulsion.
Reminder of better days before
our donnybrook destruction.

So, I celebrate alone
with no jubilant jig.
Memories of shamrock shakes
and your blarney, ever so big.

St. Pat's will pass
with whiskey, Baileys and beer.
Sorry a pinch so messed it up.
Really, Irish you were here.

2-Nitropropane

Floor cleaning time at the paint factory.
Annual event – removing accumulation of
powders, resins, polymers
and all that makes paint, paint.
Normal solvent not available.
2-Nitropropane used instead.
Kneel down, razor scraper in hand,
scoop the goo until the clean, smooth
cement floor is revealed.
Four working the factory floor.
Game of inches. Slow going.
Full day's work.
The new solvent had a pleasant, fruity smell,
different from the nose stinging,
eye-watering, chemical intrusion
used in the past.
Neal stepped outside for fresh air.
Didn't return.
Dan felt ill.
John was dizzy.
I got a skull crushing headache.
Our faces turning a morose blue.
Foreman took all four of us to emergency.
Body suffocating from the inside.
Blood gas tests ordered hourly.
Oxygen masks mandatory.
Hours later, treatment slowly showed
red blood cell improvement.
Released after observation
the following morning.
Company gave us the day off.
Paid the medical expenses.
2-Nitropropane
never
mentioned
again.

2-Nitropropane interfered with ability
of red blood cells to carry oxygen

Phone Tag

There was a time, not too long ago
when a telephone was attached
to a home, not a person.
Most homes had one phone.
Some had an extension in another room,
but same number, same line.
If you called and no one answered,
the conclusion was *"no one home."*
Perhaps someone was in the shower.
Or weeding in the garden.
Or working in the garage.
Or ignoring the phone
because they didn't feel like talking.
It didn't matter. No one answered.
You simply called back, later.
No Caller ID. No "leave a message." No text.
You just called back.
The family shared the phone.
A private conversation was rare.
Long distance was expensive.
Waited until 10pm to call California
because the rate dropped to a
dime a minute.
Did it hinder our lives?
No.
In many ways, it freed us instead.
There wasn't such a sense of urgency
of communicating right here, right now.
A scratch pad by the phone
relayed that someone called for you
while you weren't home
with a hand-written number to call back.
When you did,
you hoped they would be home, too.
If not, maybe someone on the other end
would write your number down.

Phone tag.

Procession

In the land of milk and honey
and kingdom promising –
arrives an invitation divination
to meet the king. The king!

Beginning at the procession,
lesser titles prelude.
Barons with their Baroness,
then Viscounts and their brood.

Hopefulness begins to fill.
Succession gradually proceeds.
Excitement slowly energizes
anticipation that it feeds.

Then Earls and Countesses
bring the line up faster.
Marquess and their family crest.
Duke and Duchess with their laughter.

All the while, in this noble now,
a feeling of elation.
Closer to the hearts desire.
Exuberant intoxication.

Prince and the Princess
extend their graciousness.
Nearly there, to see the host –
fulfill his own bequest.

Suddenly, it's the moment
when birds and bees both sing.
Arriving at journey's end.
The King! The King! The King!

Message in a Bottle

On a deserted island,
abundant amenities natural –
what would I choose
as a message in a bottle?

Knowing its journey
might take months, maybe years –
Would it be plea or prayer
while pursuing to persevere?

It might simply say
Tell all I'm ok...
With no concept where
I became a castaway.

Bobbing in the ocean.
Casting fate to the wind.
Plenty others better deserve
the hope it delivers within.

This is my destiny.
My kismet. My karma.
My own reason and rhyme.
My own Dalai Lama.

Is it more useful
if kept here instead?
Convenient water storage.
Message goes unsaid.

I will not cast the bottle
back into the sea.
It will not fuel my futile faith
or add to the briny debris.

Instead, I send a message
directly to myself.
Be smart. Be clever. Survive.
Play the hand that you were dealt.

Healium

Ascension
on a balloon.
Into the clouds.
Above the birds,
spires, roofs
and treetops.

The wind decides
where I will ride.
Sails open air
not knowing where.
Rising above the
bustling action below.

Escape gravity
for a while.
Especially the
seriousness
and realities
of hard ground.

Soar along –
observe from a
higher perspective.
Problems seem
so much smaller –
because they are.

My mind
drifts with the breeze.
Captured
by wonder.
Caught up in the
fascination of flight.

Love to remain
in air, forever.
Every balloon has its berth.
Drifting down from adventure.
Soft landing to the
anchorage of earth.

Healing and Hades

It's not difficult to follow doctor's orders
when feeling sore, weak, sick.
Tough part is getting better
without messing things up worse.

After three weeks, I now see
light at the end of the tunnel.
Recovery and healing –
reaching for sunlight.

Mending took much longer
than hoped for or expected.
Now, nearly accomplished –
I can ease back into life.

I cannot expect to be
the same person as before.
At least, not right away.
Takes time to get back to speed.

I regret the absence
doing all the things I love –
Part of the process.
Time stolen from me.

Moments literally put on hold.
When my body overcomes its lapse.
When my mind purges the anesthesia.
Bring my operating system up-to-date.

Healing is essential. Necessary.
Sacrifice embraced.
Sweet, sour, savory.
Part of the journey.

During convalescence –
consider the suffering. Pilgrimage.
The struggle inside and out.
Hopeful liberation from Hades.

Dream Introspection

I have a dream.
Not the kind you have when you sleep.
A dream of doing something.
Being something.
Changing something.
Building something.
Creating something.
Loving something (or someone.)

A dream is barren
until it becomes action.
If it stops before there,
it doesn't go anywhere.

A dream is a beginning.
A start.
Caterpillar
craving to become butterfly.
Dreams too
require metamorphosis.
Only then will they reach the sky.

Small dreams –
just as important
as big ones.
Perhaps they lack
peacock plumes
and a lion's roar.
But the world
might be better off
than it was before.

Sometimes
a dream becomes
the reason to keep going.
A reason to keep living.
Sharing a dream –
the secret handshake
of other dreamers –
who you may
inspire along the way.

Follow your dream.
No one else will do it for you.
In a world desperate
for solutions,
if not for dreamers,
then who?

Fat to Slim

Seen you go from fat to slim.
Eat the fruit and drink the gin.
Touch the glass and toast to cheer.
Careful control, it would appear.

They say dieting is dangerous.
Sun, too close for Icarus.
Keeping it off is really the question.
Lifestyle change, a better suggestion.

It's certainly difficult to do.
Transformation makes dreams come true.
Fabulous feeling when health takes over.
Like finding a field of four-leaf clovers.

Your present isn't perfectly thin?
Not comfortable in your own skin?
Remarkably, a new direction provides
balance where regimen and reality coincide.

Dress Regress

Shoes had little use.
Rare occasion chartreuse.

Peacock socks match the shoes.
Popularity sings the blues.

Pumpkin pants because she could.
Fashion not really understood.

Leather belt, ruby red.
How it matched goes unsaid.

Silk blouse, aquamarine.
Color combination rarely seen.

Necklace, imitation jade.
Rose ribbons tie blonde braids.

Parrot hat takes the cake.
Final straw, last mistake.

Someone, please, dress her well.
Taste in clothes really smells.

No excuse to look that rough.
Probably better off in the buff.

Tent-ative

Dad would select the site.
Remove debris and rocks.
Then pitch our family's
heavy canvas duck tent
where we all slept, together.

He dug a small trench
around the perimeter
just in case it might rain –
which it almost always did.
We called it camping.

One major tent rule
all of us had to follow –
a nightmare for active kids –
"Don't touch the inside walls,
especially if it's raining."

It was waterproof only if the
inside walls were not disturbed.
Otherwise, wherever touched,
water would begin seeping
where we were sleeping.

The culprit was easy to find.
Obviously based upon leak location
and the person directly next to it –
and a soaked sleeping bag.
Most of the time, it was mine.

Perhaps I was stretching.
Trying to capture a spider.
I just know that by telling me
NOT to do it made matters worse.
Victim of my own compulsion.

I would quietly suffer
unpleasant damp bedding –
praying it would absorb the wetness,
not create a
family uproar at 3am.

Morning would come
and if lucky,
everyone slept through
the night in comfort,
except for the wall toucher.

Towels would sop up
the puddle on the floor
and the sleeping bag
drug outside to dry.
Visual testimony to my guilt.

They make better tents, now.
Superior weather protection.
Most of all, eliminating
the childhood fear of torture
from one innocent, false move.

Camping in the canvas tent with cousins Nancy and Carl on each end and me and my sister Renee in the middle

Masquerade

Which mask are you wearing today?
Sad mask? Lonely mask?
Happy mask? Funny mask?
All meant to fool
what's really
going on inside.

Let the charade begin.
Currency
at face value.
Effective –
most of the time.
Why dig deeper?

Frightened to
reveal the real deal?
Allowing others
to see
your actual self?
Is that so painful?

Fear a mask
more attractive
than your truth?
Self-induced facade
offers others
no other choice.

You put forth
what everyone sees.
The version
you believe is better.
No one notices
it's a disguise.

Everyday,
a new dance.
New masquerade.
Another impersonation.
Until finally discovering a mask
that looks just like you.

Mask Charade

Smiley face is on today –
no one can tell I'm sad.
If I wear enthusiasm,
no one knows I'm mad.

Put on disguise.
It won't reveal.
Don't have to face
how we really feel.

Behind the mask.
Too much to bear.
Naked truth
too timid to share.

Great place to hide.
Façade. Incognito.
Designed to deceive.
Camouflage ego.

It's not Halloween.
Or a masquerade.
No excuse for
daily mask charade.

Pack away your phony face.
Demonstrate your value.
Courage without illusion.
Expose the rawness of you.

Without the mask,
you're not who they thought.
Maybe you're really
the actual one they sought.

Déjà Vu Due

Déjà vu
where are you?
Are you disappearing
as I age?

Getting older,
you should get bolder.
Doesn't experience
increase the percentage?

Once came upon me
in a town in Tennessee.
Perceived the bar was not that far –
recognized the entire village.

Of course, I had never been.
Somehow simply knew within.
An ominous feeling, déjà vu –
like speaking an unknown language.

Occurrences are less and less.
Really shouldn't get distressed.
Been to a lot more places
during the déjà vu shortage.

Déjà vu
robs me of something new.
Steals away pioneering
before I turn the page.

It's ok we don't see each other.
Sense of self will not suffer.
Being there the first time –
actually my advantage.

Losing Again

Dealt a bad hand.
Cannot catch a break.
Picked the wrong horse.
Tragic mistake.

Behind the eight ball.
Thrown a curve.
Disastrous gamble.
Lost all my nerve.

Born under a bad sign.
Black cat crossed my path.
Dire superstition.
Hopes of winning dashed.

Can't buy a vowel.
Lady luck has frowned.
Fully down and out.
Ship has run aground.

Life hands me lemons.
Pay dirt is a dud.
Pockets come up empty.
Future's clear as mud.

Praying for a miracle.
Karma visit me.
Gain a gift of godsend.
Profit to prosperity.

Spin the wheel of fortune.
Reality Russian roulette.
A game you'll always lose
and certainly will regret.

Equality

Jefferson wrote in the
Declaration of Independence
that *all men are created equal.*
Assuming he meant *"men"* as humans,
including women in the mix,
it should have read
all humans are created equal.
But we are not the same in any respect,
as I am as different from you
as you are from me.
Even though we are not really created equal,
we can wish, hope and fight for equal justice.
Equal opportunity. Equal rights.
A level playing field.
Some say the playing field should be tiered
in order to account for lack of income,
lack of a fair shake, lack of qualifications.
Perhaps the same mindset
awards a trophy to every participant,
making everyone a winner.
In truth, everyone is not a winner.
In truth, some people are
simply better than others –
in athletics, in academics, in business,
in kindness, in generosity, in thoughtfulness.
Equality cannot prop up an undeserved
without taking something away
from the rightly earned.
To me, fighting for equality
means giving every citizen a chance
to achieve inherent potential
born inside all of us.
Whether we do achieve it
is our personal responsibility.

Our Turn

You had your chance to do your dance –
form the future for us all.
Is it better? Lives improved?
Have your efforts hit the wall?
Still at war, just like before.
You don't talk about that much.
If our system's still run by you,
no wonder we're out of touch.

Such a mess you've left us in –
so many issues unresolved.
Can women earn as much as men?
Has prejudice evolved?
Do homeless have a place to live?
Do Vets finally have good care?
Why is health a costly headache
when the sick are in despair?

Infrastructure falling down,
floods and fires persist.
Better education for us all
so we do more than just exist.
Build upon the things that work –
tear apart what won't.
See our future loud and clear.
Instrumental in new hope.

It's our turn, our voice.
Step up to be heard.
Time to store old ways away –
questions now need answers.
It's our turn, it's our voice,
time to shape what life becomes.
We are our own destiny –
let's do what must be done.

Different Drummer

I played percussion
in high school band,
but I've always been
a different drummer.

I could read the music.
Yet, I preferred to
invent new parts
for the band's numbers.

It wasn't always appreciated.
Conductor more rudimental
than experimental. I was told,
"Play the part. Play the part. Play the part"

I did, when asked –
to keep grades high
and musical associates happy.
Still, scores should only be recommendations.

This different drummer
refused to conform
to many other things
besides music.

When everyone's focus
was on a Harlem Clown
who climbed into the stands –
my attention was on a pretty girl.

Not joining the lemmings
or mindlessly following the crowd.
Finding my own path
versus going with the flow.

Rock the boat.
Make waves.
Don't always go by the book
or run with the pack.

Won't spend my life
simply playing the part.
Square peg in a round hole fits.
Just not in the way round pegs imagine.

When everyone in the high school bleachers were focused on the basketball player "joining" the crowd, my mind was obviously fixated on other things...

Treading Water

A rainy, cold early June day.
Gateway Grove on Lake Sammamish.
Swimming lessons.
The day to learn how to tread water.
At the dock's deep end.
Over the head of a seven-year-old boy.
First, shown how to bicycle pedal with our feet
and use arms like wings on water.
Seven students plunged into the cold, blackness.
First time I had ever jumped into deep water.
Submerging to the depths until
struggling back to air and daylight.
A breath of air after escaping Davy Jones locker.
Treading water – more difficult than I thought.
Bike pedaling and splashing,
while losing the bobbing battle
seemed like an eternity.
Exhausted, I dog-paddled back to the mossy dock,
the security of solid refuge –
reaching my fingers onto the old cedar board surface.
The instructor barked, *"Back in the water!"*
and stepped on my fingers,
causing both surprise and pain.
Sending me sinking to the lake bottom.
Rising back to the surface,
I grabbed the top of the dock, sobbing.
"Get back out there!" she screamed.
She stepped on my fingers, again.
Collapsing into the wicked water,
heading toward the shore,
listening to the instructor berate me.
Mother saw me coming in. Still raining hard,
it may have disguised my tears.
I told her what happened.
She asked me who my instructor was.
Next class had a different teacher.
Treading water taught again.
Quickly learning from a more gentle soul.

Beware

"Beware the Ides of March,"
whispered in my ear.
What sort of caution must I take?
Whom or what shall I fear?

Keep my eyes open.
Mind my p's and q's.
Watch my step. Keep up my guard.
It's mine to win or lose.

I will take heed. Steer clear.
Stay on my toes.
Keep my distance.
Walk on eggshells, waive my woes.

Not aware what I must beware.
In fact, I do not have a clue.
Shall I worry about a stab in the back –
or worse, a personal Waterloo?

Beware. Beware.
Anything can happen. Anywhere.
Is there a cure for such paranoia?
Can I be saved from my despair?

Tell me, please tell me.
What sort of danger will I face?
"Beware the Ides" is not enough.
I need the time, the trouble, the place.

My armor. My shield.
Help me make it through the day.
Protection and security are only words
eluding those who will betray.

"Beware the Ides of March"
haunts my doubt and dread.
Shall I let the whisper rule me?
Or shall I rule it, instead?

Sirens in the Distance

Hours before dawn.
I should be sleeping.
The house, quiet.
Faint sirens
moan in the distance –

Listening closely,
I cannot tell if they're
getting closer
or further away ¬–
tearing through night's serenity.

I wonder
if someone's home is afire
or a drowning in the river.
Heeding a domestic abuse call
or helping a heart attack victim.

Maybe it's worse.
Horrible freeway accident.
Earthquake warning.
Volcano eruption.
Dam collapse.

Tsunami...
Poisonous gas leak.
Nuclear plant disaster.
Notice of imminent attack.
Perhaps a signal to evacuate.

Coyotes yowl along –
disturbs their darkness, too.
A most unwelcome duet.
Sirens do slowly fade.
Howls become yips and whimpers.

Now only clock's pendulum
competes with the calm –
comforting rhythm for my racing mind.
With a yip and whimper, I too, surrender –
seeking the solace of sleep.

Worry O'Clock

5am again.
The worry alarm wakes.
Filling my head
with concerns –
regrets and mistakes.

Sleep, I say,
return to slumber.
Change position, fluff the pillow,
pull up sheets and covers.
No matter what I command,
my vote has been outnumbered.

I lay among my ineptness
solving nothing –
answers, desperately seeking.
Awake too soon while still in bed
when I should be sleeping.

Now it's 6am and
I beg for a few more winks.
Can I turn off my busy brain –
use the minutes that still remain
before daylight becomes distinct?

Alas, the clock strikes seven –
time to rise and face the day.
All the effort I just spent –
wasted on what I now relent
when worry got in the way.

Gossip

People talk.
Dredging up
rumors and half truths
directed at the
target of the venom.

Are they embroiled
in an illicit love affair?

How could they desecrate
such hallowed ground?

When I saw them they were
as thick as buttermilk.

Perhaps it's time we
ascend our pettiness
and fret about
our own quintessence
instead of
gossiping through the grapevine
and slandering via scuttlebutt.

Take in our own dirty laundry –
wash and iron
our malicious behavior.
Set the cycle on permanent press
and drench away
the muck, the sludge, the grime.

Incompatible

Not your obedient servant.
Ship sailed long ago.
Pretense to understand
impossible's not apropos.

Used to be a sparkle.
Attractive admiration.
Blossom fragrance began to stink –
I was anti-altercation.

No romantic dinner.
Vacant stores to shop.
Real as geese teeth.
We were just a flop.

Nothing really in common.
Unfunctional apparatus.
"I'm not to blame," you exclaim –
when there never was an *"us."*

A Twinkle

First, a twinkle
in a father's eye.
A body develops
frail and small.
Protecting the fragile spirit
for terrestrial birth.

The body grows. Sprouts.
Thrives. Bigger. Taller.
Stronger vessel
for the spirit within –
where it, too,
expands its horizon.
Increases insight.
Gains new ground.

Over time, the body ages –
becoming frail like before.
Yet, the spirit continues
to cultivate the soul.
Expanding. Evolving.
Flourishing until
its final moments.
Leaving earthy anatomy
joining the stars to become
a twinkle, once again.

The Snake

Don't speak with a forked tongue
nor slither, wriggle or crawl.
Born the *Year of the Snake*
without any reptilian features at all.

The Chinese view of the zodiac zoo
is much different than one might think.
Philosophical. Organized. Intelligent.
Intuitive. Attentive. Distinct.

Never been cold blooded.
Have teeth where a fang graces.
Fact is, I'd be closer to a beaver
without four years of braces.

I identify with the view from Shanghai
and wear the symbol around my neck.
Won't shed my skin but will look within
and discover my serpentine introspect.

This Ain't Heaven

Sometimes we have to
remind ourselves –
this ain't heaven, yet.

There'd be no tears
or spears
or jeers
or smears
or fears –
if heaven's
saintly lessons were
planted and growing here.

Until there's no terror.
No error.
No unfortunate twist of fate.
No seize of life and property.
No dread. No pain. No hate.
Until we can learn
to leave what we can't forsake –
we dare to fulfill our prophecy
of war and ruin and ache.

We can strive to make it better.
Remove the unveiled threat.
Deal with changing things
we'd rather just forget.
Provide sympathy and kindness
to a world still quite upset.
Realize, it's no surprise
that this ain't heaven, yet.

In Praise of Persistence

If at first, you don't succeed,
try, try again. Then try some more.
If they say it simply can't be done,
time to place them on ignore.

Endurance. Tenacity. Stamina.
Headed toward resolve.
Enthusiasm shan't be extinguished.
Spirit remains enthralled.

Pluck and perseverance.
Determination and dedication.
Fortitude takes the mighty reins –
drives closer to vindication.

Edison invented the light bulb
after three thousand tries.
If he had surrendered to the folly,
he wouldn't have found the prize.

If you want something badly enough,
let nothing stand in your way.
Make persistence be your insistence.
With your heart, you shall obey.

Pioneer

Pulling up long, deep roots –
planting them in fresh earth.
Sowing seeds of hope.
Homesteading new rebirth.
Bravely enduring hardships.
Confidence from a sturdy spine.
Forging the future frontier
while leaving the past behind.

That pioneer spirit
lives deep inside me.
To lead, not follow.
Create versus comply.
Blaze new trails triumphantly.
Do instead of try.
Keep on moving forward.
Always look ahead.
Start what I will finish.
Freshly bake the bread.

Pathfind my purpose.
My actions. My fate.
The brave heart
of the pioneer
is also mine innate.

Footsteps

Footsteps in the sand.
Temporary impressions.
Momentary permanence.
Short-lived evidence.

Footsteps which
guide the next ones
wishing to follow
the path.

Even though
footsteps fade –
trampled by others –
Set direction. Set the route.

And the contribution?
Remembrance,
long forgotten.
Yet, passage remains.

Life's mission –
creating
paths of wisdom
for future travelers.

100 years from now,
who remembers
pioneers
who blazed the trail?

Previous
presence on earth.
Souls floating
above the sand.

It doesn't matter.

Continuing to move forward.
Looking back at who's behind.
There comes a time
when neither is no longer.

Farm-to-Table

As a small child I learned
where meat comes from.
We had our own cows
and I accompanied Dad
to the butcher shop.

White walls.
White overalls
and lab coats.
Shiny stainless steel tables,
sinks, saws and grinders.

Meat was the primary color.
Steaks were cut and hamburger made.
Individual packages wrapped
in white butcher paper.

Each package
carefully stamped
in red ink
describing
contents within.

Butchers were friendly.
Efficient. Clinical. Hygienic.
Discussing weekend fishing
as they went
about their business.

Never had to observe
the actual kill.
Bullet to brain –
gently corralled
at my grandfather's farm.

But I knew about it.
Frightened cattle
make bad meat.
One of the
farming facts of life.

Gave me perspective
few people have today.
Greater appreciation
of the
farm-to-table process.

I do know where
meat comes from.
The meat counter
at your local grocery
is where it ends up.

Hereford at my grandfather's chicken and cattle farm, circa 1959

Silence of the Plants

What if
plants scream when cut?
Maybe they simply want to
remain alive, just like us?
Ultrasonic sounds
human ears can't hear.
Perhaps a silent whimper
when corn on cob is sheared.
Wonder what carrots feel
pulled from their earthly bed
cut, trimmed and peeled?
Strawberries sliced and chopped
suffer their desperation mute?
Do we make melons moan
when scooped, carved or cubed?

Certainly, it's something
Vegans don't want to know.
Their desired food of choice
no longer apropos.
If broccoli is off the table.
Mushrooms absent from the list.
Kale can be curtailed.
Dates and figs desist.
Lettuce and legumes –
not a salad make.
I would assume this awful news
would make their diet quake.

They worry about fish and fowl.
Other meats forsaken.
Might change with consciousness
learning every living thing can ache.

Man Affect Destiny

Coal power plant.
Water level low.
Rising temperature.
No evanescent foe.

Oceanic currents.
Change of climate.
Eco-collapse.
Creator reassignment.

Frightened society
begs protection.
Hurriedly pushes
partisan election.

Gloves are off.
Ready to fight.
Hell bent to survive.
Merciful might.

Needs more than polish.
Or even a patch.
Nature bleeding
from many a scratch.

Go to the airport.
Fly into space.
Profit before progress –
deafening disgrace.

Cast out fate,
face elimination.
Too little, too late –
our preservation.

Black Licorice

Somehow daughter
got the idea
I LOVED black licorice.
Especially the semi-hard kind.
First as a Father's Day gift.
Then birthday.
Then Christmas.
With smiles
and warm wishes
that accompany
giving and receiving.

Not my favorite.
Quite low, actually,
on my treat totem pole.

Son caught the clue
and began to include it
among his gracious gifts.
A large licorice inventory
stacked up.

It was tricky.
On one hand,
I didn't want to appear
non-appreciative and
hurt feelings.
I felt guilty saying thanks.
It had to stop.

Year later,
while all together,
I mustered up courage
to confess
I was simply being polite
all along.
Please, no more
black licorice.

To my surprise,
daughter blurted out
"I don't like Easter Peeps, either"
Goes to show
there's a difference
between indulgence
and integrity.
Life lesson
learned later.

I enjoy red cherry licorice
occasionally –
especially the soft, stringy kind –
probably containing
no actual licorice at all.
Not on my wish list, though.
I'll just buy it for myself
when I get the hankerin'.

Buttercup

We lay on the soft green lawn while
she places a buttercup at my chin.
"You love butter," she says.
Which I do, I admit.
But how would a flower know?
More likely, it's a retort.
Retaliation from being plucked
from its flower family for
the purpose of my preference.
She could have said,
"You're a bugger,"
which would have been as true.
Now the poor buttercup
is obligated to
simply share its blossom
until each petal is plucked
from the
puppy love child's play
of *"love me" – "love me not."*

Go for the Jocular

Make ‘em giggle.
Make ‘em laugh.
Make ‘em snort
like a goofy giraffe.

Tell a joke.
Crack a smile.
Clown around
a little while.

Bit of whimsy.
Comic relief.
Turn frowns upside down.
Make grins from grief.

Bring on the levity.
Sharp wit, gentle jest.
Wisecracks, hoodwinks,
humor and happiness infest.

Either be a wet blanket
or strive to be enchanting.
One thing that’s for sure –
no one’s ever died laughing.

Ponderous

Red wing blackbirds twirl their call
perched upon pond reeds, large and small.
Blue Heron holds court in the shallow –
casts an eminence sovereign shadow.
It's a peaceful kingdom, after all.

White swan discovers a cool reception –
no hospitality for foreign perception.
Few days' rest, then wings flutter south
to other waters without a joust.
Next time a permanent selection.

Gaggle of Canadians claim residence
as if it was their heritance.
Mallards and Mergansers coexist
like pleasant pacifists,
avoiding major subsequence.

Autumn day's cinema –
ticket to nature's plethora.
Reds and golds, unwoven wicker –
reflection in countryside mirror.
Resonance from the outdoor orchestra.

Pond de León

A Great
Blue Heron walks among the
Cattails.
Ducks
Enthusiastically dunk their
Feathers in replenishing water.
Geese, too, fly in from the
Heavens,
Imitating fighter
Jets,
Kamikaze
Landing on a
Millpond aircraft carrier.
None are friends with the
Opossum on the shore or
Perch in the pond, each accusing ducks of
Quackery.
Red wing blackbirds' piccolo
Song establishes each bird's
Territory,
Updating the most current
Vacancies among the
Weeds and brush.
Xenial act to do for others.
Yonder lagoon, a natural
Zone for wildlife appreciation.

Bird Song

Long way home.
South bound.
Nests in tree.
Flute sounds.

Song for sun.
Song for moon.
Glee for free.
Sweet tune.

Deer hear.
Frogs heed.
Toot sweet.
Chirp deed.

Sound color.
Share song.
Rest with ease.
Sing long.

Light of day.
Miles to go.
Rise to fly
where wind blows.

Winter Jailbreak

Spring me out
from winter's cruel cooler.
Help me seek sanctuary
in butterfly gardens
and ladybug lairs.

Hatch a plan.
Generate a buzz.
Sprout a scheme.
Watch the breakout bloom
into penitentiary pastels.

Get my raincoat
and galoshes ready
to dance in April's showers.
I'm ready to escape
on roller skate wheels.

It's liberation
closing winter's cell door,
thanks to nature's pardon.
A palpable parole of yellow.
Let the dandelions roar.

Actor and Verse

Pretend you're a poet.
Just one afternoon.
Writing before you know it –
let your flower bloom.

May not be Frost or Keats.
Tennyson or Shakespeare.
Don't fear it's incomplete –
or if too amateur.

Character you're playing –
bard, not balladeer.
No further explaining
or rules to adhere.

Write for yourself.
Therapeutic healing.
Mental, emotional health –
dealing with your feelings.

Pretend you're a poet.
Portrayal may come true.
Talent's where you grow it.
Something you never knew.

My Instrument

Some play piano.
Or saxophone.
I play words.

No secret to it, really –
converting an idea
into something worthwhile.

A jazz musician efficiently
selecting which notes to play
as well as the space between.

For me, the attraction is
creating something new
from finite components.

Spade in the ground.
Dig in. Dig up. Explore.
See what's there to find.

Will it make me famous?
More likely a footnote.
But it won't trample my satisfaction.

Not inventing a
new drug for cancer.
Just a melody of words.

Which I orchestrate
to establish a connection
with myself and others.

One Second Decision

Quick.
Swift.
Pronto.
Choice.
Done.
Set.
End.

Wake
or not.
Break
or not.
Take
or not.
Make
or not.
Ache
or not.
Fake
or not.

In
a
wink.

One
second
shapes
a
lifetime.

Forges
fate.

Computer Calamity

When my trusty computer
develops an operational issue,
it greatly disturbs me
and drives me berserk.

My peaceful pleasant world
turns way upside down.
Obsessed with this hideous problem.
Can't leave it alone.

I believe I can fix it.
Search internet culture for solutions.
See if anyone else has the same flap.
Or if my issue is unique.

Turn the computer off and on
a dozen or more times
hoping it fixes itself.
Supreme pain in the ass.

Try this. Try that.
Find the convict causing
all the trouble.
While I turn a nasty shade of magenta.

Then I cowardly confess to myself –
it must have been my doing.
Can it be undone?
Trial and error reveals the answer.

Finally, it returns to its old self
until next time it throws me a curve.
A good reason why, however,
I'm not trusted to work on cars.

Exacerbation

Treatment for my love disorder.
Placebo a no go, healing a hope so –
Correct cardiovascular defect.
Produce therapeutic effect.
Subcutaneous injection
without adverse reaction.
Still got you under my skin.

Pitter patter arrhythmia.
Coronary angina.
Cardiac amnesia.
Only want to please ya.
Atrial fibrillation –
feasible fabrication.
Don't want a broken heart.

Remedy my recovery.
Calculated cautery.
Elixir for immune response.
Serum for our renaissance.
Chronic infatuation.
Prescribed reciprocation
unties my gastrointestinal knot.

Wrong Side of Right

"A sane person to an insane society must appear insane."
– Kurt Vonnegut, ***Welcome to the Monkey House***

They called him crazy.
Demented. Deranged.
Daft. Delirious.
Insane. Lunatic.
Screw loose. Bonkers.
Crazed. Cuckoo.
Erratic. Unhinged.
Bats in the belfry.
Nutty as a fruitcake.
Mad as a March hare.

Yet, he was correct
and the whole world askew.
Words fell on deaf ears.
Misunderstood.
Science wouldn't see it.
Logic didn't believe it.
Truth denied.
Right or wrong,
it didn't make
a damn bit of difference.

When black is white,
wrong is right,
green is red,
behind – ahead,
naked truth
must adorn attire.
While in Rome,
blend in. Curtail.
Odd one out
rarely prevails.

Butte Camp

Put the tent up.
Fix the flap.
Guard food from
bear attack.

Discover nature.
Take a swim.
Capture the moment –
a perfect win.

Grant yourself time.
Don't let it go unused.
Latch dreams together.
Allow room to improve.

Leave it as you found it.
Carefully douse the fire.
Know where you go next?
If not, simply inquire.

Addicted to Pickleball

Would play every day if I could.
For health reasons, I need it.
Best exercise I've ever known.
Two hours pass under
pickleball's spell –
as if only a few minutes.

Game caught fire
throughout the land.
Baby boomers.
Young and old.
In my opinion, it inspires.
Kindles my flame.

Sister and brotherhood
full of comradery.
Sharing the obsession.
Embracing its enchantment.
Fun at every skill level.
Addiction with positive results.

Jonesing for the next game.
A delightful disorder.
Withdrawal when I can't play.
Impatiently waiting
for my pickleball fix.
No rehab necessary.

Moment of Measure

Moment taken to simply breathe.
Ponder the should – and should not – believe.
How influential contamination infects
the very information one collects.
Each stone, each brick, mortared, depicts
a foundation dependent upon what was picked.
Illusion of strength by what appears
may not stand when the soul is sheared.
Thoughts we choose, words that affect –
the ones we keep or willfully reject.

Wiener?

Gone the innocence.
Gone the time you could serve
a hotdog to a lady
without sexual inference.

Just a tube steak,
when it comes to being frank.
It's a man-eat-dog world,
feeding the hand that bites it.

Feast on this footlong,
I double-dog dare you.
Until we meat again,
relish today, ketchup tomorrow.

Frank Furter

One Last Wink

Postscript:
The wink you give as you walk away.
– Shaun Usher

Incidentally.
By the way.
While on the subject.
Apart from.
An aside.
In as much as.
With reference to.
Speaking of.
A related matter.
In passing.
One also notes.
Luckily.
As a side effect.
Interestingly enough.
Fortuitously.
By way of explanation.
Anyhow.
Moving on.
On another note.
By chance.
Now then.
At the end of the day.
As a general rule.
Push comes to shove.
In the long run.
When all is said and done.
In the final analysis.
All things considered.
Everything being equal.
Given the circumstances.
One more thought.
I digress.

Poems of the Pandemic

I selected these poems, written during the Covid-19 Pandemic, to illustrate my thoughts during this historical human event. They are in order of when I wrote them and left the dates on each one on purpose.

The pandemic created a permanent scar on the planet, with an impact not seen in more than a century. I lost both healthy and compromised friends to the disease. It will remain one of the most significant developments in our lifetime.

I hope, in a small way, these poems may provide insight for future generations as to the state of mind of those who lived it.

Edmond Bruneau

The New Normal

It will come to pass,
this virus we now face.
People will once more
embrace with a hug
or deliver a firm handshake.
We'll travel again
to broaden our horizons.
But for now, our new normal
means closed doors.
Cocooning. Isolation.
Fear of unknowns.
Panic over a cough
heard at the supermarket.
It is cold season after all.
Although
one can't be too careful.
Wash hands at
every opportunity.
Cancel upcoming events.
And wait.
Wait until we get the word
of better news bearing
a release from exile.
No one knows how long
this new normal will be.
I've got a feeling
we better get used to it.

Edmond Bruneau
March 18, 2020

Waiting for the Bomb

I remember the Cuban Missile Crisis.
A breath away from nuclear devastation.
Teachers told us to duck and cover.
An alarm would sound and
we'd seek safety under our desk.
A terrible time for young souls
trying to comprehend the horror
and finality at such an early age.

Perhaps it was the same
in my parent's generation
when Pearl Harbor began
the second war to end all wars
with the sacrifice of rations
and rubber drives.
Likely, their youth was also hardened
by the fear of the unknown.

What we survive makes us stronger.
Tempered, creating stronger steel.
Like a vaccination
helping us to endure
the next fear on the horizon.
We were more ready for it
because of World War II
and the Cuban Missile Crisis.

And today, the 2020 Pandemic.
Some of us have the antibodies
from living through a crisis before.
The rest, even young souls
have now lost their innocence
embedded with new fear of the unknown.
We will get past the point of
waiting for the bomb.
It will change us.

Edmond Bruneau
April 4, 2020

NOT Chicken Little

The sky is not falling.
Nor do I live in fear.
Already living through
a damaging heart attack,
ischemic stroke and multiple sclerosis –
I am one with existing conditions
and potential target for Covid-19.
I'll be 67 in August.
I'd like to see 68. And beyond.

But I would also like
my retirement account –
scrimped and saved
over the last half century –
to retain a good portion of its value.
But that's not what happens
when a government prints more dollars.
Money becomes worth less.

So, here we are,
walking the tightrope.
The balance of restarting
our economic engine versus
the practicality of
safely sheltering in place.
The longer non-essential business
is shut down, the greater the need
for government to support citizens and businesses
with money it really doesn't have.

We need to examine both sides
of the coin quite seriously.
It should not be a matter of
essential versus non-essential.
It should simply be a matter of safety.
And if a barber can cut hair or a
restaurant serve fewer patrons with precautions –
they should be allowed to do so.
If you don't want to get a haircut or go
to a restaurant then don't.

When Churchill was asked to cut arts funding
in favor of the war effort, he actually never said,
"then what are we fighting for?"
Someone made it up.
But it's still a valid thought.
It's been a month of sheltering in place.
It's time to consider what are we sheltering for –
and if there will be a functioning world
in which to return.

I'm NOT Chicken Little.
And the sky is not falling.
I will have to take greater safeguards than the
majority without compromised immune systems.
Eventually, I want to hug my son and daughter,
grandkids and dear friends again.
I want an ice cream cone at the fair.
Sit next to a stranger at a live concert
without worrying if I'm signing my epitaph.

People will get sick. And like the common cold,
there never may be a cure.
Let's get the economic ball rolling again
for all our sakes
and with caution, concentrate on
reducing the number of deaths with Covid-19 –
not only the number of cases.

Edmond Bruneau
April 23, 2020

Civil Disobedience

Instead of ripping off
the bandage
in one painful stroke,
we are removing it slowly
in four different phases
each spaced at least
three weeks apart.

A little bit at a time
just so it won't hurt so much.

Meanwhile, hospital workers
are being furloughed.

Hairdressers jailed.
Prisoners early-released.
After all, we have to make room
for the crime of civil disobedience.
Feeding one's family
under penalty of law.

It's not the bandage
I worry about
but the growing infection
underneath.

People who would rather
earn money themselves
than become beholding
to their government tossing
scraps and tidbits their way.

And prevented work until Phase Four.
Or rather, not allowed
to make a living for themselves
until then.

By then,
the roast is burnt.
The ship has sailed.
The train has left the station.

Bills can't be paid.
Drowned in debt.
Bankruptcy
goes for broke.

Meanwhile, creating criminals
out of the very people
who made what our country
the prosperous nation we once were.

Something is very wrong.

If the cure is worse
than the disease,
which should we choose?

When we question
these desperate actions
of civil disobedience
and ask why they occur –
the answer lies within
our own collective fear.

And the painful impact
of its economic destruction
with
the blood
on our own hands.

Edmond Bruneau
May 8, 2020

It Shouldn't Happen Anywhere

Peaceful protest
is an American tradition.
It can help lead to change
a person's heart and mind,
social attitudes
and laws we live with.
The Boston Tea Party
was a protest about
taxation without representation –
with a lot of tea sent to the depths
of Davy Jones Locker.
Woman's suffrage – a protest
about equality and
the female right to vote.
Fast forward to Vietnam –
protesting a war
many regarded as unnecessary
unjust and unwinnable.
Four dead in Ohio
became the movement's mantra.
The peaceful protests
inspired by Martin Luther King
lead to major changes
in civil liberties
and segregation.
In these times of tribulation,
leaving millions of
hard working people
unemployed and fearful
of an invisible disease –
is it any wonder a video
of law enforcement
clearly using
unnecessary lethal force
became a tipping point
for outrage?

It's not just one thing,
it's a thousand things
stirring up
the level of frustration
and the criminal acts of
looting and violence.
Good things do not come from
destroying property and
stealing shoes and televisions
under the malfeasance of justice.
Clearly, it gets our attention
but not in any kind of positive way.
A peaceful protest against police brutality
can ensure individuals responsible
for their heinous use of authority
receive the punishment deserved.
Burning and looting will not.
Fact is, how really different are
the perpetrators
stealing and destroying
under the guise of a protest
than the individuals they are protesting about?
Both are criminal.
Both are wrong.
Both are things
that shouldn't happen anywhere.

Edmond Bruneau
June 1, 2020

Change My Mind?

Social media –
no longer social.
People,
with way too much time on their hands
have become
missionaries of their own truth.
Evangelistic in their zeal.
Posting their opinions.
On politics. On police. On safety.
On virus. On education.
From both sides of the spectrum.

And no matter how many
posts one does a day,
it's not going to sway my beliefs.
It's not going to change my mind.
I'm not going to wake one day
and realize the error of my ways
thanks to your continual input.

Frankly, it's turned
into a pissing contest.
It's stunk up what used to be
a fun way to connect with
friends and relatives.
Anniversaries. Birthdays.
Vacations. Celebrations.

Now, today,
before I see or read
anything I truly want to
embrace or enjoy –
I must scroll past a litany of
posts designed to
educate me with
a lopsided point-of-view
with the clear intent
of making me believe
what they believe.

Honestly, it tells me more about you
than I ever really wanted to know.
I have friends on both sides of the aisle.
and we usually keep it that way
by discussing everything but
all this urine on social media.

Yes, I know it's your right
to proclaim your opinion.
Evidently, it's also your mission
to pollute what used to be
a wonderful social media oasis.

Realize this.
There's a good chance
no one is going to change your mind
about anything you strongly believe in.
And there's an equal chance
your persistent posts
won't change mine, either.

All your work,
all your efforts,
all your memes
may very well be in vain.

If we spent as much time and effort
daily working on messages of love,
joy, kindness and understanding,
perhaps it just might make
our world a better place.

Instead of the cesspool
social media has become.

If you feel I'm wrong, please –
don't try to change my mind.

Edmond Bruneau
July 19, 2020

Everything in Life is Alive

This is the year of the cicadas –
insects emerging from the soil
every seventeen years.
This is also the year of Covid-19.
A virus emerging from nowhere.

Yet, there are so many things
we don't understand about it.
In the natural order of things,
all life has a beginning and an end.
If it didn't we'd still be fearing
the bubonic plague.

So, maybe Covid-19 is alive
and even without a vaccine
it, too, could have a life and a death.
Or at the very least a
much less threatening mutation.

We can only hope
this infection wasn't done
on purpose.
Like the British General attempted by
purposely issuing smallpox-exposed blankets
to Native Americans in 1763.

Perhaps it wasn't spread.
Perhaps it was *"hatched."*
Not on our blankets,
but on our new TV,
cell phone and
coffee table.

If true,
we did this all to ourselves
because we wanted cheaper
and bought cheaper
from another land
far far away.

Maybe, besides destroying
U.S. television manufacturers,
U.S. phone factories
and U.S. furniture companies,
we got more than
we bargained for.

The 2020 pandemic.
Let us hope, at the very least,
like the cicadas,
It too has a cycle –
hopefully greater than
every seventeen years.

Edmond Bruneau
August 10, 2020

How Can You Possibly...?

It's political.
One side believes
there is no good
to come
out of the White House.
The other side
believes it will lose
more than the race
if the opponent wins.
In every presidential year,
red and blue
are always like this.

The difference today
is the lack of deference.

It's one thing to take pride
in your choices.
It's even fine to share what you think.
But when you call someone
an idiot
for not agreeing with your point of view,
that's where I call foul play.

"How can YOU possibly
believe in...?"

"Anyone who believes THIS
is THAT!."

Let the characterizations begin.
Amped up and out of control.

I wonder
how many decent relationships
will be ruined by this new disease
called *'My Way or the Highway'?*

No matter what the demagoguery,
I have a clue for you.
It's not as black and white
as you believe.

Edmond Bruneau
August 21, 2020

Virtual Venue

Flung into
being an actor
in a video game
of my own creation.

That's me
on the LCD –
a formation of pixels
red, blue, green.

Technologically –
a miracle.
We've become
Jetsons now.

Not only myself,
but friends, family
and companions
play the game, too.

Used to be,
I could touch,
smell, even taste
human contact.

It gave purpose
to my viability.
Subtle nuances by
actually being there.

Now it's virtual.
Virtual classes.
Virtual vacations.
Virtual visits.

Accessing it all
on a phone,
tablet or
computer screen.

It this is what life
has now become?
An electronic reality?
An artificial intelligence?

It's a flat screen
without dimension.
Without disposition.
Without a soul.

Yet, I deliver myself
to this devil device
creating some contact
with others in the world.

By choice?
Not really.
By necessity?
Perhaps.

It's better than
the vacuum of isolation.
Better than nothing is
no satisfying achievement.

Call me old fashioned.
I enjoy being in the room
with others with the
same inclinations.

Live.
Without a wizard
crafting a sub-reality
in a manufactured world.

One day
I fear I will fall completely
into the looking glass
and never find my way out.

Edmond Bruneau
November 13, 2020

"Water, water, everywhere,
And all the boards did shrink;
Water, water, everywhere,
Nor any drop to drink."
– Samuel Taylor Coleridge, ***The Rime of the Ancient Mariner***

Home for the Holidays

It's Covid's fault, first and foremost.
Cursing the 2020 holidays with its fear
and common sense protectionism
preventing any sort of family affair
to transpire
feasting on remaining bones
of turkey past
in our solitary confinement
without son, daughter,
son-in-law, daughter-in-law
and grandchildren
ages five and seven,
all redefining what
Christmas was
into what Christmas is
with the pandemic panic
being the only visitor
coming down the chimney
on Christmas Eve,
stealing away
the merriment
and fellowship
of family
celebrating another year
of bountiful blessings
and garbage bags
full of ribbons and
torn wrapping paper
while giving the song
Home for the Holidays
a much different meaning
than was ever intended.

Edmond Bruneau
November 29, 2020

Desiderata Revisited

Amidst all the clamor and commotion,
realize peace is possible when you quiet your mind.
Be kind. Live authentically. Speak sincerely. Listen well;
everyone has their story.
Avoid loudmouths who overwhelm your voice.
You are you –
no need to measure against another's yardstick.
Take pride in your talents and accomplishments.
Pursue things you love doing –
work which brings you joy.
Safe is sedentary. Take risks – be willing to fail.
Failure is only a step behind success. Keep your wits.
Don't be a sucker.
Love yourself. It's a prerequisite to loving anyone else.
You are wiser than yesterday.
Welcome wisdom with age.
Keep inside the spirit of light
when dealing with darkness.
Misfortune is part of life. Shit happens.
Dwell on the positive.
There's a new day tomorrow.
Allow yourself tenderness and compassion.
Like every other lifeform on earth, you deserve a place.
Beware of Chicken Little claiming the sky is falling.
If it's supposed to fall, it will,
without your worry or concern.
Let the universe unfold. Pray to a greater power.
Uncover your peace.
On this sphere plagued with pandemics,
climate change, war and weariness,
it's still the best place we know about.
You are blessed to be here.
Give a smile to someone who needs it.
Pay it forward.
Celebrate your humanity.

Edmond Bruneau
January 7, 2021

Sour Grapes

It was the simplest of
reciprocal relationships.
I'd design your wine labels
and you would send me wine.

Obviously, I wasn't
doing it for the money.
Not when the main objective
is to drink one's profits.

We began the arrangement
twenty-four years ago
when I created
the first of many designs.

A handshake
was all I ever needed.
With our forty year friendship,
why require anything else?

Your merlots and cabernets
garnered numerous awards.
People loved the grapes
grown on the lakeside shore.

You once told me
another wine maker
offered you a million dollars
for the brand I created for the blend.

I had hoped our comradery
would continue to mature
like the fine wine you create.
With new flavors and textures as it aged.

We never spoke of
what my work would have cost
in the real retail world.
You were always generous with the wine.

Until you weren't.
So here we sit.
A pandemic.
And plans to sell the winery.

Three years of design
unaccounted for.
The irony you teach accountants
is an unfathomable betrayal.

I've been trying to encourage you
to do the right thing
for more than two years now.
You stopped communicating in July.

How very sad it has come to this.
Now that I'm no longer an asset,
your appreciation has
now become depreciation.

It's partially my fault.
I believed your promises
when I shouldn't have.
I believed in our bond.

I will not beg.
Especially for something I earned.
A deal is a deal.
For me, the handshake was real.

Nothing backed up in writing.
I sit cellared, cool and dark, aging.
Without recourse.
While our wine becomes vinegar.

Edmond Bruneau
January 30, 2021

www.ingramcontent.com/pod-product-compliance
Lightning Source LLC
Chambersburg PA
CBHW040303170426
43194CB00021B/2884
* 9 7 8 1 9 3 6 7 6 9 0 3 2 *